Projects to Get You Off the Grid

Projects to Get You Off the Grid

Rain Barrels, Chicken Coops, and Solar Panels

Selected by Instructables.com, Edited by Noah Weinstein

Skyhorse Publishing

Skyhorse Publishing books may be purchased in bulk at special discounts for sales promotion, corporate gifts, fund-raising, or educational purposes. Special editions can also be created to specifications. For details, contact the Special Sales Department, Skyhorse Publishing, 307 West 36th Street, 11th Floor, New York, NY 10018 or info

Skyhorse® and Skyhorse Publishing® are registered trademarks of Skyhorse Publishing, Inc®, a Delaware corporation.

Visit our website at www.skyhorsepublishing.com.

10 9 8 7 6 5

Library of Congress Cataloging-in-Publication Data is available on request.

ISBN: 978-1-62087-164-5
Ebook ISBN: 978-1-62636-230-7

Printed in China

Disclaimer:
This book is intended to offer general guidance. It is sold with the understanding that every effort was made to provide the most current and accurate information. However, errors and omissions are still possible. Any use or misuse of the information contained herein is solely the responsibility of the user, and the author and publisher make no warranties or claims as to the truth or validity of the information. The author and publisher shall have neither liability nor responsibility to any person or entity with respect to any loss or damage caused, or alleged to have been caused, directly or indirectly, by the information contained in this book. Furthermore, this book is not intended to give professional dietary, technical, or medical advice. Please refer to and follow any local laws when using any of the information contained herein, and act responsibly and safely at all times.

Table of Contents

Introduction

There is no better way to become self-sufficient than to get free energy and water from the sky, and free eggs from chickens housed in your own backyard. *Projects to Get You Off the Grid* showcases twenty-one exceptional step-by-step projects around the themes of solar and wind power, rainwater collection, and raising chickens. Each project is authored by an expert with a strong desire to share their knowledge and contains multiple images and written instructions to help you follow along, step by step. Let these projects inspire you to make your own green infrastructure to get you off the grid and become more self-sufficient.

All of the projects in this book are from Instructables.com. Instructables is the most popular project-sharing community on the Internet, and part of the Autodesk family of creative communities. Since August 2005, Instructables has provided easy publishing tools to enable passionate, creative people to share their most innovative projects, recipes, skills, and ideas. Instructables has over 80,000 projects covering all subjects, including crafts, art, electronics, kids, home improvement, pets, outdoors, reuse, bikes, cars, robotics, food, decorating, woodworking, costuming, games, and life in general.

—Noah Weinstein

Editor's Note

The wonderful thing about Instructables is that they come in all shapes and sizes. Some users include hundreds of high-quality pictures and detailed instructions with their projects; others take the minimalist approach and aim to inspire similar ideas than to facilitate carbon copies.

One of the biggest questions we faced when putting this book together was: How do we convey the sheer volume of ideas in the finite space of a book?

As a result, if you're already familiar with some of the projects in this book, you'll notice that selected photos made the jump from the computer screen to the printed page. Similarly, when dealing with extensive electronic coding or complex science, we suggest that anyone ready to start a project like that visit the Instructables' online page, where you often find lots more images, links, multimedia attachments, and downloadable material to help you along the way. This way, anyone who is fascinated by the idea of converting a car to run on trash can take a look here at the basic steps to get from start to finish. Everything else is just a mouse click away.

* Special thanks to Instructables Interactive Designer Gary Lu for the Instructables Robot illustrations!

Backyard Chicken Coop

By robbtoberfest
(www.instructables.com/id/
Backyard-Chicken-Coop/)

I made this little chicken barn a few years ago to house three to five laying hens in my back yard. I'm in town and had to design a "pretty" one to keep people from having a chicken coup. This one was inspired by some Kansas barns I've seen. The total cost was about $40 when fully completed. Chicken wire, some 2 × 4s, and damaged siding were the costs. Damaged siding is half price at my local lumber store. Other things I used were scrap wood from old bathroom cabinets, leftover hardware, paint, and wood from house projects, plus a lot of scraps and hardware from a condemned house down the street (I got permission to take things before

they bulldozed it). Shingles were given to me by my neighbor, leftover from roofing his garage. There are some basic rules for designing and running a good healthy chicken shack:

1. Adequate floor space per bird.
2. Dry with good ventilation.
3. Temperature control.
4. Predator protection.
5. Keep it clean+fresh water/ food=happy and healthy birds.

Many towns actually allow up to five chickens but no roosters. Check local rules on this if you plan to build. If you do get chickens in town, be courteous to the non-chicken majority so the rest of the city chicken people don't get punished through politics and zoning. I submitted pictures of this coop to someone who was working on a coops book a while ago and they included a picture of it in *Chicken Coops, 45 Building Plans for Housing Your Flock*, by Judy Pangman. Sources for my chicken knowledge: *Building Chicken Coops* by Gail Damerow; The City Chicken; Raising Backyard Chickens; Feathersite; and the

Poultry Page. I recently posted another coop, a chicken outhouse with a beer can roof at diylife.com.

Step 1: Floor Space, Framing, and Nest Boxes

My floor space includes the exterior run. I knew I wanted three heavy egg layers, so from the charts I used 10 square feet per bird rule. There are different suggestions in different books/guides; there is a pretty good chart at Virginia Cooperative Extension. I built this 18" off the ground to create a shady part of the pen underneath the coop. The floor is 2 × 4s framed like a little porch 3 feet by 4 feet sitting on 4 × 4s attached with many 3" screws. The walls are just under 4' tall and I used 3" screws to put together the 2 × 4s. Four-foot walls are a good dimension because siding and plywood come in 4' × 8' sheets. I framed in the next boxes here. I think a rule is one box per three to five laying birds. They like dark, comfy places to lay. Making the boxes the size of a 12" dustpan works great when cleaning the coop. Many books suggest elevated boxes, but these floor boxes have worked great for three years now. Avoid treated lumber inside the coop or where they perch; the toxic stuff can affect the birds (i.e. sickness/death).

Step 2: Roof

I don't have many step-by-step pics for this so you'll have to use your skills to fill in the gaps. I cut 2 × 4s with angles to make three sets of rafters and attached them with 3" screws. I screwed down some old cabinet wood across the rafters to make the roof, leaving a little 4" hole near the center peak for a cupola. Then I shingled the roof leaving the center peak hole open. The cupola is made like a little bird house that sits over the vent hole. Use a hole saw to make holes in its sides and staple window screen on the inside to keep out the critters. Attach it with 3" screws. This helps meet rule #2: Dry with good ventilation.

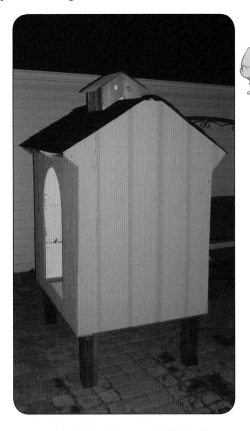

Step 3: Walls

Cut the siding to fit the framing and attach it with nails. Use a jigsaw to cut out doors and other openings; save the cutouts for building the doors. Keep the following in mind while designing walls: Make openings for windows; this is important for summer heat control. Build walls tight to keep out wind and drafts; this is important for winter cold control. This is a standard chicken coop rule: Have good ventilation but no drafts.

3

Step 4: Doors

A main door for you to access the coop and a small chicken door are the only doors really needed. But I added cabinet doors, a nest box door, chicken door and a main door on this thing. The hinges I used were from old bath and kitchen cabinets. The main door was made with old porch flooring. Boards were attached diagonally to the siding cutout with nails; then I used the jigsaw to clean it up around the outside. This made the door look more old fashioned. The nails will stick out the back side; bend them over or cut them and grind the stubs smooth. The other doors were made directly from the siding material and some trim wood. I just attached hinges and handles with some trim around the edges. The trim is important to close the gap where the saw cut the siding. I added some plastic near the top to shed rain over the cabinet doors.

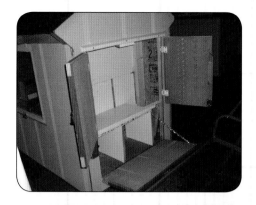

Step 5: Finishing Touches

Add the roost perch for night time. Make a perch out of a 2 × 4 with the edges rounded a bit. Under the perch make a place for the droppings to gather. This roost area is usually the only place inside of the coop where the droppings are, which makes cleaning easy. (Don't use treated wood!) When I finished the coop, it ended up being very heavy, so I attached some boards to the bottom and used a hand truck to wheel it (with help) to its home location. The run/pen can be made easily with 2 × 2s and 2 × 4s as seen in the pic below. I enclosed the top of the run to keep the hawks out. I later added a matching run on the opposite side when I added some more hens.

Step 6: Extra Notes

I've changed the coop a little over the years to allow for more birds. I've removed the storage area and added a roost in its place. Also, I've removed the small pen and made a large run for the birdies.

Clipping Chicken Wings

By Noah Weinstein (noahw)
(www.instructables.com/id/
Clipping-Chicken-Wings/)

Chickens can't fly as well as other birds, but they can flap their wings enough to carry them over fences and out of the coop. If you've got backyard free range chickens, clipping their wings is a must so that you chickens don't escape and get lost, or worse, like coming across an angry dog or some other predator in the area. Clipping chicken wings is a bit daunting if you've never done it before, but once you've clipped a wing or two, you'll discover that it really isn't as difficult or dangerous as you may have thought.

Materials
- Clean pair of sharp scissors
- Towel (optional)
- Pliers (optional safety measure)
- Corn Starch (optional safety measure)
- Gauze or rag (optional safety measure)

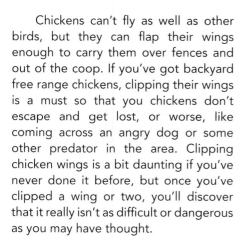

Step 1: Catch a Chicken

The hardest part about clipping chicken wings is catching the chicken. Some chickens are docile and like being touched, others fear humans and run away like their lives depend on it (which I guess they do sometimes). A few things that seem to help is to corner them in a small space so they have less of an area to get away from you. You can also use a towel and throw it over the chicken. That should slow them down long enough to grab them. Once you grab the chicken, you should gently apply pressure to their wings and pick them up, or you can go for the pro maneuver and snatch them up by their ankles. Watch out for their claws and beaks. The more regularly you handle your chickens, the easier it will be to catch and hold them. So for some chickens, this may be a non issue, but for first timers, it's a little challenging.

Step 2: Invert and Calm the Chicken

Once you have caught the chicken, spend a minute calming it down. Pet it softly, make cooing noises, and, what seemed to work best—invert it. When the chicken is upside down, it goes into a trance and becomes much more docile.

Step 3: Expose the Wing

With the chicken upside down, identify which wing you are going to clip. Expose what are called the primary flight feathers by grabbing the chicken's wing and gently pulling it away from its body. You can tell the primary flight feathers from the other feathers on a chicken's wing because they may be a different color, are generally longer, and are the ten or so feathers closest to the tip of a chicken's wing. Many people find success by clipping just one wing. Others clip both wings. The theory behind clipping just one wing is that the bird will be thrown off balance enough by having just one smaller wing that its flight capabilities will be drastically limited. It seems that chicken owners have not reached consensus yet on this issue. We cut back the feathers on only the chicken's right wing. This way they're all the same, and when we need to cut the wings again in a few months, we can be consistent with what wing we'd like to cut.

Step 4: Cut Back the Primary Flight Feathers

Using a clean pair of sharp scissors, clip around two-thirds of the length of the first ten or so feathers on the chicken's wing. Take a look at the diagram below to see roughly how much of the feather you should be cutting off. You can also use the chickens secondary flight feathers (located in the same position on the wing as the primary flight feathers, just closer to the chicken's body) as a guide. The idea is to cut off a significant amount of the feathers, while not making a cut so close to the chickens wing that you make them bleed. Chicken feathers have blood veins extending into them about an inch or so. If you cut below this point, the feather is completely dead, the chicken feels nothing, and the wings get clipped successfully. If you cut above this point (closer to the chickens body/wing) the chicken will begin to bleed through the cut feather and your chicken will be in danger. If that occurs, apply pressure to the tip of the feather with a rag,

and get your chicken to a veterinarian. Corn flour or starch applied to the cut feather cuticle can slow the bleeding and help the chicken clot. Additionally, grabbing the base of the feather with a pair of pliers and removing it completely from the chicken wing can also help the chicken clot. This process will hurt your chicken, but in a pinch, it may save its life. Apparently the veins in the feather itself just don't clot very well. If you cut the primary feathers carefully, there's no reason why you should ever cause your chickens to be in pain or to bleed during this process.

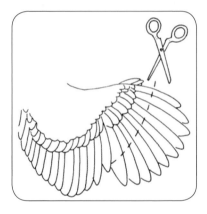

Step 5: Release the Chicken

Once you've trimmed the chicken's feathers, release the chicken. It might be a little disoriented for a moment, but it should be unharmed.

Small Chicken Tractor for the City Dweller

By Jrossetti

In this Instructable, I'll outline the requirements for a small chicken tractor for the backyard chicken enthusiast, such as myself, and describe the process of building it. After seeing a lot of chicken tractors on the internet for outrageous prices, I decided it'd be better for me to build a cheaper one myself that fit my needs a bit better. I'll show you how I did it and give some pointers on making your own design.

For those of you who don't know what a chicken tractor is, it's essentially a chicken coop that can be moved around. Some of the main purposes for a mobile chicken coop are to allow the chickens to fertilize the grass (though this isn't pretty at all), eat the grass (keeping it trim if done right), and eat bugs and weeds, and so it is easy to hide when your parents come to visit. There's other benefits too, though I'm not saying a coop is *not* the way to go (my city actually has an ordinance stating any permanent chicken coop must be forty feet away from any human house, so a tractor is a nice, efficient way to bypass that ordinance).

A lot of what went into my design is the direct result of trial and error and the input of the very knowledgeable people over at www.backyardchickens.com.

So let's begin.

I started the project with the following goals:

- Small enough to be moved by hand around my property
- Big enough to comfortably house one to four chickens
- General protection from the elements (sun, wind, rain, etc)

- Protection from predators
- Easy access to the things I need to access

And of course, the following elements were required:

- henhouse (where the chickens could sleep at night) with proper ventilation
- nesting box (where they lay eggs)
- covered run area (chickens don't like sun tanning, or standing in the rain)
- food and water support for at least one day

So moving on to the first step we'll take a look at the design.

Step 1: My Tractor Design

From the intro, we have a general list of what we need to include in the design to make it successful. This list is the absolute bare minimum I would suggest any chicken tractor or even a chicken coop should include to make the upkeep easy for you and reduce worry.

Size and Construction

I wanted a tractor big enough for my chickens. I started out with three chickens but may have as many as four or five. Most sources on the Internet agree that chickens need a minimum of 1 square foot of indoor space and 2 square feet of outdoor space to live, and, of course, any more than that and they're even happier. So based on that math, I'd need a henhouse size no smaller than 4 square feet, and a run no smaller than 8 square feet. I can do that!

I ended up on dimensions of 3 feet wide, 7 feet long, and about 4 feet tall at the highest point. That is about 21 square feet of run space, and the henhouse is 9 square feet (3' by 3') and is about 3 feet tall at the highest point.

Most of the frame will be made using 2" by 2" pine, the base frame from 2 × 4s, and the rest with whatever is cheapest.

Protection from the Elements

Now, with that list in hand, my next consideration is the environment the tractor will be in. In my case, it's all level ground with a mix of bare ground (the garden area), grass (lawn area), and concrete (driveway and side yard). I also have fruit trees and shade trees. The weather is hot and dry in the summer and snowy in the winter, so we need to take all of that into consideration in designing the tractor.

So, it's pretty much a given that with all the different types of ground the tractor can travel on, we'll need wheels. A sled-type of setup won't work too well.

Chickens don't do too well in the sun, so they'll need shade. They'll get that with the trees in parts of the property, but not all, so I need to design a roof that will cover the run area of the tractor. And since it snows in the winter, it's probably a good idea to slant the roof to shed the snow (and rain in the spring time).

So I decided a roof slanted towards one end, made from PVC roofing, is probably the cheapest and easiest solution.

The base of the tractor is made with redwood, which is more water resistant than pine or normal construction materials. Plus, I didn't want to use any chemically-treated woods, as if the chickens peck at it they might get sick.

Protection from Predators

I want it to be heavy enough that it can't be moved by any 'normal' predator (dogs, cats, raccoons, etc). But I also want it light enough to move by hand. I also want it to be able to repel entry by most predators, so I won't be using chicken wire! I don't want any opening larger than about 1 square inch (even though I'm sure mice can get in that anyway, I just don't want anything larger squeezing in).

I will be using 1/2" hardware cloth for the sides, screwed down with big screws and washers, so it can't be pulled out easily. Any doors will be secured with bolts or safety hooks, so most predators won't be able to get in.

Ventilation

The most important part of the henhouse is ventilation. There's plenty of material out there on the net describing the dangers of improper ventilation in a henhouse and what you can do to mitigate those dangers. I am of the opinion that more is better, so I designed it with that in mind.

The whole inside wall is open to the outside, with a removable panel that covers the lower portion in the winter. The upper back of the henhouse is a hinged vent panel, so I can open it wide in the summer and close it more in the winter.

Easy Access

I want to be able to easily access the food, water, and nesting box in order to top off the food and water and take eggs. Also, I want to be able to easily get into the henhouse for cleaning, and the run area for the same reason. I additionally want to be able to open and close the henhouse door from the outside.

So I've kind of integrated the waterer and feeder into the design since I don't have a lot of space to work with. We'll take a look at those in the next couple of steps.

The Decision

So, with all of this in mind, I will construct the tractor using wood, hardware, cloth, some PVC roofing and whatever other bits and bobs I find along the way that I need. The design went through a few different revisions, but here's a couple of pictures of what the final design looks like.

I have the final plan available in Google Sketchup format for those wanting exact dimensions. You'll find it on step 5 of this Instructable.

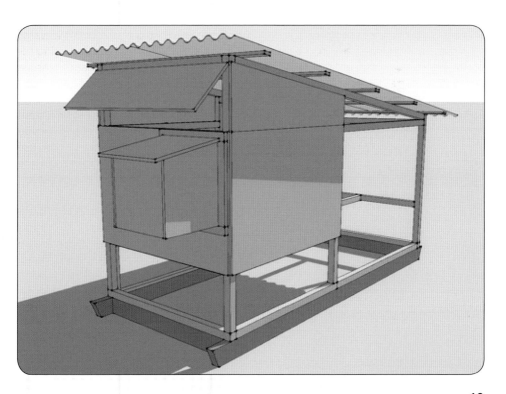

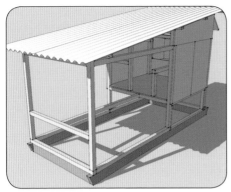

Step 2: The Waterer

Normally, a watering system for chickens consists of a hanging waterer. They usually take up a lot of space and are messy because the chickens can get water everywhere. I didn't want that and don't have a lot of space to waste on it, so I opted for a nipple system, like what's used in the bigger chicken factories. The nipple waterer is very efficient, gravity fed because it relies on very little pressure, and is actually pretty easy and cheap to implement.

I got my nipples from TekSupply. They also have a version that is a push-in type. These work better for how I used them, but this is a DIY-as-you-go type of project so you might have better luck with the others. In any case, I bought a handful of each just in case.

The nipples are plugged into 3/8" ID Vinyl tubing, which is plugged into a 2-gallon bucket that sits on a little shelf up in the side of the henhouse. I have two of them in this setup: one inside the henhouse and one outside down in the run area. The TekSupply page for the nipples say they don't require a drip cup, and, for the most part, that's true; but keep in mind that most chickens are partially psychotic and I've seen them get water all over the place even with these little things. So you may want to consider getting a drip cup if yours are consistently messy.

One other thing to keep in mind is that you want at least 12 inches of height between the nipple and the bottom of the water supply, so you can get at least a couple psi to keep the nipple from dripping.

The bucket is more or less in place. I can easily remove it should the need arise. I just need to detach the tubing from the bucket when I do. It's easily filled using a plant watering can with a long spout; mine holds enough to fill it half way. Win!

Winter Problems

When I filled it with water to test it in the winter, I noticed it'd freeze up. I solved this by putting a 50 watt aquarium heater into the bucket, and kept the nipples from freezing by placing the inside nipple immediately next to the small radiant heater I'm already using to add a little warmth for the chickens. You'll see what I'm talking about in a photo attached to the last step.

The outside nipple I keep from freezing using a small 35 watt halogen reflector bulb. It keeps it warm enough to do the job and sheds a little light so the chickens can see what they're doing, if that's even remotely important.

plugged it into a reducer with a couple of elbows, and strapped it onto the side of the henhouse, with the working end sticking through the hardware cloth. The chickens dig it. It's not quite big enough that more than one can eat at a time, but they're generally amiable and will wait—or will shove somebody aside so they can get to it.

I spray-painted it to add some UV protection because ABS doesn't play very well with sunlight.

I put cheap caps on the ends to keep bugs out while I was building it. The lower cap I'll probably stick back on whenever I'm moving the tractor to keep feed from going everywhere and whenever I fill it. The upper cap I keep on all the time, to keep the mice out.

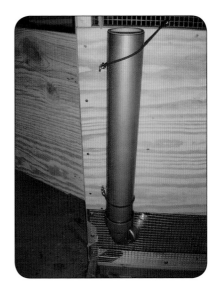

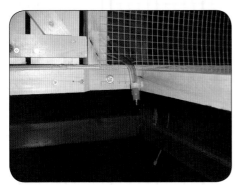

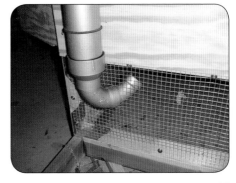

Step 3: The Feeder

I also didn't feel like I had a lot of room to put in a regular feeder, so I built my own. I built it using black ABS pipe. I obtained a 2' length of 3" pipe,

Step 4: Construction

I constructed the whole frame using standard 2 × 2s, 2 × 4s, and gold screws. I used some brackets and doodads where I thought it would help with stability.

Check out the pictures to see how it all went together.

After I got the basic frame put together, I added the henhouse floor, worked on the nesting box, and got the henhouse all put together before adding the hardware cloth/mesh sides. You'll notice I used some plastic mesh on the top of the run area and henhouse both; it's much lighter than the steel stuff, and since the chickens are unlikely to ever come in contact with it, it doesn't need to be as durable. I fastened it in the same way, though, with big screws and washers for support.

The henhouse door has a spring on the back side to keep it closed when it's supposed to be. It opens by pulling on that chain, and is kept open with a long bolt that's slid into the two eye bolts, one on the door and one on the frame. The same eye bolt is used to "lock" the door shut at night. Yes, there is space in the door pieces, mostly for ventilation, but also because it looks cool.

The upper rear vent window uses clear PVC roofing. That's for light inside the henhouse, but also because I had some spare clear PVC leftover from another project and this was a perfect fit. I can look into the henhouse and see what the girls are up to with disturbing them too much.

Speaking of PVC roofing—I attached the PVC roof using small screws and "sealing washers." These are washers with a rubber gasket on one side. Once I got it all fastened down, I tested it out with the hose, and yep, it's waterproof.

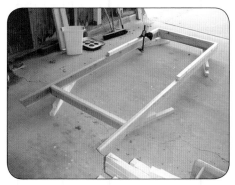

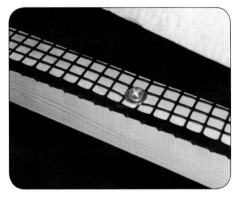

Step 5: Finishing Touches

Well, it's all put together, and now the chickens are chilling out in it. I've added the roost to the henhouse, and put a little "lip" on it to try to keep the bedding in place. The roost is actually another sub-assembly—it's attached to a piece of plywood that screws onto the actual henhouse floor. This is so that I can remove the roost and floor entirely for a couple of different reasons: easier access to get inside the henhouse in case I change my mind about the watering system or need to do any work; for easier cleaning of the floor under the roost (it has 2 to 3 inches of pine bedding underneath it, which I figure will serve about a month before it gets tossed into the composter and new bedding is put down).

I've also added a ramp up to the henhouse door. The chickens spend 99 percent of their time outside, but I think it's because they're pretty dumb creatures and haven't figured out how to jump up inside yet. They have a natural tendency (like all birds) to sleep in the highest possible location, so I'm still scratching my head as to why they'd sleep down in the run when there's a nice cozy roost to sleep in. Maybe this ramp will help out. Sorry, I don't have any photos of it.

The Final Word

I'm sorry if I haven't included specific dimensions for some parts and some of the assemblies here in this Instructable. I figure that if you download the Sketchup file, you can use the measuring tape tool in it to measure stuff out. But anyways, I just wanted to show how easy it is to build something like this, and I'm sure if you're going to build your own you'll come up with your own plan, or use mine as a general template and work your way from there.

A Word About Cost

I started this project with a goal of spending less than $250 for the whole tractor. In actuality, I spent about $270 or so. I *could* have spent a whole lot less by scavenging wood, but that wasn't a consideration at the time. Most of the expense was in the wood. The PVC roofing was rather cheap; I used two pieces at $10 a pop. And were I a better hand at construction, I could have done without all the little angle brackets and stuff.

 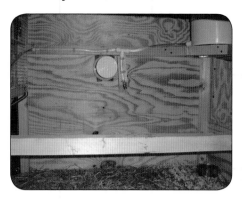

Author's note:

   I used 3/8" plywood for everything but the inner floor. Originally the inner removable floor was 1/2". I've made a few modifications to the tractor since then – now I've got a single piece of 3/4" plywood with linoleum for the removable floor, it adds stability for the roost, and is easier to clean. But the walls and other plywood bits still are the original 3/8".

   One other change I might point out – the vinyl roofing is OK, but after having this up for a few months, I don't think the roofing will last. It's already slightly warped in some spots and while it's still keeping out the rain, it looks ugly. If you are ok with the extra weight, or don't plan on moving the tractor often/ever, you might want to consider using a metal roof. It's cheaper, more durable, and will keep the sun/heat out better in the summer; on the other hand, it's heavier.

Chicken Barrow

By Sarah Noce (scmtngirl)
www.instructables.com/id/
Chicken-Barrow/)

I call this a Chicken Barrow instead of a Chicken Tractor because it really reminds me more of a wheel barrow than a tractor! Anyway, after researching chicken tractors in-depth online, I finally decided on the "hoop house" design and am very pleased with how it came out. I think this is a good project for someone with little to no building skills, and it's easy to get your friends to help because they want to know what it is! I enlisted the help of some girlfriends and my carpenter husband, who offered a lot of advice for my project and helped us end up with a perfectly square frame and very solid final structure. For example, I probably would have used galvanized nails, but he said pre-drilling and using screws is the way to go, which makes sense, but I would have never thought of that myself. Additionally, I'm pretty sure you could get away with a structure that was not perfectly square, but it certainly made it easier to align the PVC. I wanted something relatively heavy to deter predators from trying to move/lift it, so 2 × 4s were used (and because we had some on hand). A smaller dimension of wood could be used if you think predators are not as much of a problem. We have raccoons, coyotes, mountain lions (rare, but chickens might attract them!), and dogs and cats (including my own) that freely roam the neighborhood. We already had a 3' by 6' sheet of plywood in the garage, as well as some 8' 2 X 4s, so we decided to make mine 3' wide X 3' high X 8' long to minimize waste.

A few things still need to be added:

- On one end, we will use a jigsaw to cut out a door (and attach it with simple hinges) as well as two wheels. The wheel bolts I bought to attach the 6" ball-bearing wheels are not long enough to attach to the 2 × 4s, so I will need to find longer bolts at the hardware store, which is why we did not attach them yet.
- On the other end of the barrow, we will add a nesting box with a hinged lid (for egg gathering) made out of plywood as well as two handles for maneuvering the barrow. The handles will also act as extra support for the nesting box.
- I will attach two 4' 2 × 4s to the ends of a piece of tarp to provide the chickies with shade in the summer and wind protection in the winter.
- Both the hinged door and the hinged lid of the nesting box will be secured with padlocks to deter the opposable thumbs of determined raccoons.

I plan to get four chicks. I think they will be quite comfortable!

Materials/Tools Needed

- six 8' 2 × 4s (three to be used uncut for long pieces, and three to be cut down into smaller cross braces and diagonal braces)
- one 3' by 6' piece of 3/4" plywood (can fit into a non full-size truck!)
- twelve 1/2" pipe straps
- six 1/2" pieces of PVC cut into 8' lengths by your local hardware store
- about 20 feet of welded wire (you will have some left over—use it for garden cages)
- about 20 feet of chicken wire (ditto)
- lots of galvanized 2.5" deck screws
- cordless drill gun
- cordless screw gun
- jigsaw
- circular saw (optional)
- at least an afternoon's worth of time!

Step 1: Cut the Plywood Ends

We first cut the piece of plywood in half and screwed both pieces together so they could be cut with the jigsaw at the same time. Then, using screws as a guide, we carefully bent the PVC, following the edges of the plywood, and then fastened the ends with two pipe straps for safety. We used a pencil to trace the shape of the PVC. We removed the guide screws (but not the screws holding the two pieces together) and cut through both pieces of plywood with the jigsaw. We then unfastened the remaining screws and set the two pieces aside. Note: We ended with a flat portion at the top of the curve of the plywood, which ended up being useful later.

Step 2: Build the Frame

We used two 96" (8') 2 × 4s for the long ends and two 34 5/8" 2 × 4s for the short ends (which takes into account the true dimensions of 2 × 4s so we would end up with a frame that was exactly 36 inches wide to match the width of our plywood). My husband cut the short end pieces with the circular saw because he's fast and I'm afraid to use it. We added three more 34 5/8" horizontal cross braces to the rectangular frame. These add stability and double as roosts for the chickens! We then squared up the frame and added diagonal cross braces. Every connection was pre-drilled and screwed using two 2.5" galvanized deck screws. It is easier if you have two guns: one for drilling and one for screwing.

Step 3: Take a Break . . . Then Connect the Plywood Ends

We took a short break. My dog thought the barrow was being built for him. Next, we attached the plywood end pieces—again, pre-drilling and using screws. I think we used three screws

25

on each end. We attached another 96″ 2 × 4 as a center support and recessed it below the tops of the plywood ends by a half inch to account for the width of the 1/2″ PVC piping that would be bent over the top.

Step 4: Add PVC Supports

We measured the distance needed between each PVC pipe to accommodate six pieces spaced evenly apart and then screwed twelve 1/2″ pipe straps to the frame according to our measurements.

I think they were spaced 27.5" apart. We snaked the PVC pipe into one end and then the other and cut off the excess with the jigsaw. I accidentally bought one 3/4" pipe strap, so we pre-drilled and screwed that end into the 2 × 4 since it was loose inside the strap. We later on decided to pre-drill and screw all the PVC ends, just in case the pipe straps became weak. We also pre-drilled and screwed the tops of the PVC pieces into the top support piece. I didn't think to buy six additional pipe straps for this top piece, but I think the screws will hold it in place just fine.

Step 5: Cover Your Barrow with Wire

I decided to use both welded wire and chicken wire as a cover for my chicken barrow. The welded wire has the strength that chicken wire lacks, but the chicken wire is smaller than the welded wire to keep out grabby raccoon hands. The welded wire came in 4' width, so even though the long 2 × 4s are 8', I forgot to account for the depth of the plywood, so two pieces of welded wire didn't quite cover the length of the barrow. Each length of welded wire was stapled to the plywood ends, leaving a small approximately 2" gap in the middle of the barrow. However, I figure that I'm covering the whole thing with chicken wire anyway, so the gap probably isn't a big deal. It was easiest to turn the barrow on its side to staple on the wire. We wrapped the wire all the way around the bottom of the frame, but not so much that the sharp edges stuck out beyond the width of the frame. My hand was pretty sore after all the stapling. We finished stapling the chicken wire, so now all we need to do is cut out the door, attach the door hinges, attach the wheels, attach the handles, and build a

27

small nesting box. That will have to wait until next weekend, though, because it started raining. I will also cover one half of the barrow with a tarp secured by 2 × 4s to provide shade and shelter for the chickies!

Collect Rain Water with a Wine Barrel

By Mallie (chout)
(www.instructables.com/id/
Collect-rain-water-with-a-wine-
barrel/)

I think I read all of the Instructables about collecting rain water. Finally decided to build my own with a wine barrel because I didn't want to destroy the look of my future-to-be terrace. I always found rain water collectors super ugly. It's usually an old plastic tank or barrel; handy but not very pleasing to the eye (and I didn't have the motivation to build something like this to hide it). Anyway, here's how I did it.

Material

- a wine barrel (found on eBay for 50 EUR). Make sure to get one with a lid and a cork (usually it's a special cork located in the belly part of the barrel).
- a rain water collector to hook up to the gutter (found on eBay for 19 EUR, but otherwise available in nearly all DIY shops). I chose this model because the collected water would come out via a little tube and not an "open-air" half-pipe
- driller
- flat wood drill heads
- some screws
- an old piece of board about the length of the barrel's lid
- a handle

Step 1: Prepare the Barrel's Lid

Usually the lids of wine barrels are a bit wobbly. They are made of planks inserted into each other and are supposed to be inserted in a groove at the top, inside the barrel. Because of that, I had to make the lid stronger so it would not wear out from frequent usage. I found an old piece of wood board in my garage and screwed it tight at the back of the lid. I made sure to use rustproof (INOX) screws. In order to be able to close the barrel and properly put the lid back on (and because the lid is round), I had to saw the four corners of the board as you can see in the picture. Last year we bought a new kitchen and we received two extra handles (don't ask me why), so I've decided to use one of them for my barrel. The screws that came with the handle weren't long enough to go through the thickness of the lid, plus board attached at the back. So I used a flat drill head to make a wider hole and reduce the thickness so I could properly attach the handle. Make sure to place the handle in the middle of the lid; it's not only more beautiful but also easier to manipulate when you open/close the barrel.

Step 2: Connect the Rain Water Collector on the Gutter

I followed the instructions that came with the PVC rain water collector (rwc) to hook it up to one of my gutters. It was super easy; I just had to saw an 8cm section off the gutter at the right height and insert the collector. *Important!* In order to prevent an overflow and avoid my barrel to be overfilled, I installed the rwc a bit lower than the top of the barrel. Therefore the water in the barrel can't go higher than the height on the gutter where the water is collected. I drilled a large hole with the wood flat drill head, inserted the transparent tube that came with the rwc, then used silicon (same as for a shower tub or bath) to seal it and make it waterproof. That way the water could flow back via the tube should it reach a certain level in the barrel.

Step 3: Here Comes the Rain

Within one week my barrel was full to the top (I was even surprised by how much water I had in just a week). I now use it to water my plants and flowers, to wash my terrace, etc. There's still a little bit of wine smell when you open the barrel, but that's more a positive point than a negative one.

Roughneck Rain Barrel

By DonnieDillon
(www.instructables.com/id/
Roughneck-Rain-Barrel/)

Tools
- utility knife
- scissors
- staple gun
- pliers
- screwdriver

This afternoon I went to the hardware store, spent $38.22, and came out with everything I needed to make a roughneck rain barrel. My plan is to use the water I harvest from my roof to water my plants and my chickens, wash the car, and fill up my squirt guns. It was fun and easy and took less than two hours to complete and made me feel very green and environmental-ish.

Parts and Tools

Parts
- 1 32-gallon Rubbermaid roughneck trashcan (from my garage)
- 1 roll of window screen (on hand from fixing the patio door last summer)
- 1 90' hose ($15.00)
- 1 nozzle set ($3.00)
- 1 set of three-conduit locknuts ($0.99)
- 2 half-inch boiler drains ($9.48)
- 4 flat metal washers ($2.10)
- 4 rubber washers ($5.32)
  Total with tax: $38.22

Step 1: Attaching the Faucets

1. Begin by using the utility knife to cut a hole in the trash can for the faucet several inches from the bottom of the can, but be careful not to make the hole too big. The rubber washers will keep any of your harvested rain water from leaking out of your barrel.
2. Thread the metal washer onto the faucet first, then the rubber washer. The rubber washer should be sandwiched between the metal washer and the side of the trash can.

3. Place the faucet through the hole you cut and put another rubber washer on the inside of the trash can.
4. Use the pliers to help screw the locknut on tightly. The tighter the screw, the less likely there will be leaks.
5. Repeat this process for the second faucet several inches from the top of the trash can. While a second faucet probably isn't absolutely necessary it can act as an overflow valve.

Step 2: Attaching the Screen

The screen is important. It will keep debris out of your rain barrel. It will also keep mosquitoes from being able to get in and lay eggs in your water.

1. Lay the screen over the top of the trash can.
2. Begin stapling the screen to the top of the trash can. Be sure the can is clean inside before you staple it closed.
3. Use the scissors to trim off the excess screen.

Step 3: Making the Lid

I don't suppose a lid is strictly necessary, but I think it makes it look a little better, and it will keep debris from piling up on top of your rain barrel. Using the utility knife cut out an opening in the lid of the trash can. This will be the intake for the downspout from your gutters. Put the lid on over the screen and your rain barrel is complete.

1. Begin by cutting your down spout to the desired height. I used a utility knife, but I suppose a Dremel tool would work too. You may need to move a couple of the brackets that hold the down spout to the wall. Just unscrew them and move them where you want them.

2. Reattach the curvy bit at the bottom of the down spout and set your rain barrel underneath.

   I attached a hose to the faucet at the bottom of the barrel and ran it around the side of the house to the front where I need it, but you could just as easily skip the hose all together and save yourself $15.00.

Step 4: Installing the Rain Barrel

The last step is installing your rain barrel.

Green Solar-Powered Water Barrel

By Daniel Moeller (damoelid)
(www.instructables.com/id/
Green-Solar-Powered-Water-
Barrel/)

A green way of using rainwater with the convenience of city water. The attached solar regenerated pump enables you to water plants with pressure, even when the water in the barrels falls low enough that it barely passes the level of the faucet. The sun-warmed water also aids in the growing of plants as it does not shock them. The twin 85-gallon barrels are raised onto a very sturdy 4 × 4 box assembly from recycled wood, held together with new carriage bolts because the total weight of all the water when full is approximately 1700lbs. This frame is resting on eight 2"-thick, 18" square cement pads to prevent sinking. The barrels are raised to increase the head pressure and decrease the work load on the pump.

Step 1: Water Supplied from Mother Nature

Link barrel to downspout. Be sure that the top of barrel remains below level of water entry. I found the Watersaver attachment for the 3 × 4 downspout pipe works perfectly. In order to enable adequate water flow to the barrel, I adapted the Watersaver attachment by drilling out the side and adding a flange for a 1" PVC fitting. I sealed this by using a rubber gasket and additionally using a silicone sealer. Ensure there is a downward slope between the downspout and the barrel entry.

Step 2: Overflow Back to the Downspout

Ensure you have a complete path for water from the downspout to the barrel or barrels and then from the overflow to the downspout again. Use 1" PVC overflow line from the last barrel back to the downspout. Ensure you maintain a drain angle towards the downspout or sediment could collect in the line.

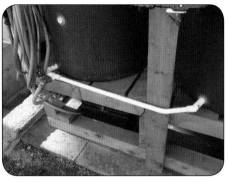

Step 3: Downspout Drain Connection

One-inch PVC entry back into the downspout. Ensure PVC pipe does not fully block the 2" by 3" downspout and keep the downward slope to the pipe to make the water flow towards the downspout.

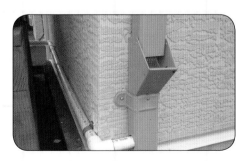

Step 4: Manifold

Common connection point for using water. This photo of the manifold is before I put the water gauge on (shown on intro and last step).

Step 5: Water Filter

Filter the water from the barrel to protect the pump. This keeps the roof sediment from wearing out the pump. This water filter will last forever, as it has a reusable nylon mesh filter inside that only requires periodic rinsing.

Step 6: Battery Box with Power Switch

Keep the battery and pump protected from the elements inside a full size battery case.

Step 7: Inside View of Battery Box with Motor

An inside view of the standard size battery case and equipment layout. The solar cell was left with clamp connections in order to enable quick removal of the battery case lid for cleaning and maintenance. The pump was recycled from an older sailboat. The battery is a standard size lawn tractor 12V, and with proper maintenance should last six to ten years before needing to be recycled at the depot. An older car battery that just doesn't have the power to crank the car fast enough anymore would be more than adequate for this application and a great alternative to buying a new battery. The 5.5W solar cell was also recycled for a fraction of its original cost from an online classified, and solar cells have a lifespan of approximately fifteen to twenty years. I wanted this little project to last as long as possible before needing any repairs.

Step 8: Flowjet Pump

Close up of Flojet 4405-143. Another pump that I have seen that is almost identical to this is made by Shurflo. This type of pump is used in RVs or sailboats to supply water pressure, as well as for using as a wash down pump on boats. I chose this type because it has an internal pressure switch that stops it from running all the time, only turning on when the water pressure in the hose drops. In addition I got a super deal on it secondhand. There are many different styles of pumps available that will be more than adequate for this application. It depends on your budget and the availability of secondhand pumps in your area. Other things to consider would be whether or not you want the pump running all the time (lawn sprinkler) or only when you press the trigger on your hose nozzle. Without a built-in pressure switch, the pump will run whenever the power is switched on. In all types of applications, make sure the pump output pressure does not exceed the pressure rating of your hose/pipe or it might burst if the outlet closes or becomes blocked unexpectedly.

Step 9: Water Gauge

As the water level changes inside the barrel, the level inside the tube will follow the same level. This was fun to install as I didn't want to waste all the nice rainwater and drain the tank before I drilled a 3/4" hole in the bottom of the tank to install the angled shut-off valve. I reminded myself to only use a battery powered drill. I reused some half-inch plastic tubing that I had left over from another application and connected it to a 3/4" angle valve with a shut off (which came in handy during install). I sealed around and under all penetrations into the barrel (valve and screws) with a two part epoxy

that was a waterproof filler and sealer.
It is important to not completely seal
the tube or the level will not change to
reflect the level in the barrel.

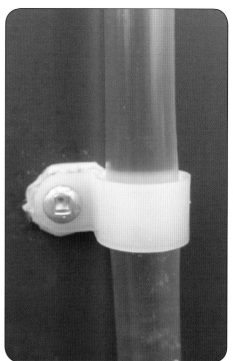

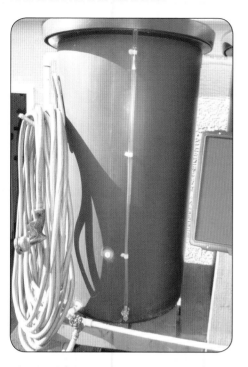

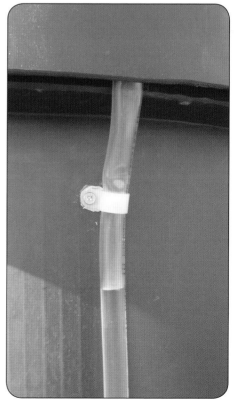

Rainwater Collection and Distribution System

By Mark Shannon
(mark11photography)
**(www.instructables.com/id/
Rainwater-collection-amp-
distribution-system/)**

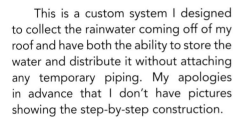

This is a custom system I designed to collect the rainwater coming off of my roof and have both the ability to store the water and distribute it without attaching any temporary piping. My apologies in advance that I don't have pictures showing the step-by-step construction.

Get Your Materials and Tools

It's a pretty simple collection of materials, most of which can be found at your local hardware store. I did a little hunting around to find an appropriate rain barrel and ended up getting one from an eco-store here in Calgary.

Materials
- (6) 2 × 4 studs (each 8 feet long)
- approximately (100) 3" long deck screws
- 55-gallon rain barrel
- sections of 2" central vacuum tubing (could substitute plumbing PVC or ABS pipe, but they cost two or three times the price). Length is determined by the distance you need the water to travel—I needed six sections.
- assorted couplings, end caps, 90 degree elbows, 2" ball valve, one 'Y' section, and two threaded adapters to connect into the rain barrel.
- 2" plastic straps to affix the pipe to the fence.
- (1) 10' length of 3" PVC pipe and assorted 3" couplers/elbows
- Silicone caulking
- stainless steel screws (optional, or substitute the deck screws)
- PVC/ABS Glue
- C-shaped straps—number depends on the length of your delivery pipe

Tools
- power drill
- saw (I used a mitre saw, but a hacksaw would work)
- measuring tape
- level
- string

Step 1: Build the Stand

I didn't have any set plans, but I knew I wanted to build something that wouldn't fall apart under the weight of the water-filled barrel. A 55-gallon barrel of water weighs over 200 kilograms. Also, if the base sags, the connections will be stressed, so make the base of the legs wide to support the weight. I built mine out of 2 × 4s, roughly 2' by 2' by 2'. The barrel I purchased (which can be obtained quite inexpensively, just make sure what they used to contain wasn't toxic) had a spigot attached, so I had to accommodate that during construction. I had to be careful to make sure the lengths were correct (measure twice, cut once), and that the joints were square. Take a bit of extra time and it will stand up much longer.

Step 2: Prep the Pipe

In this step I prepared the lengths of pipe by drilling a 1/2" hole every foot along the pipe—be sure that they are all in line.

Step 3: Determine Your Fall Line

I have a 40' section of fence I wanted the pipe to travel, so I put a screw in the fence at the level the water would be exiting the barrel, and then a second screw in the fence where the pipe would end. I then took a string and attached it to both screws to find out what the fall would be from the barrel. From this line I put marks on the fence where I would attach the pipe using the straps.

Step 4: Attach the Pipes to the Fence

I attached the pipes to the fence with some plastic C-shaped straps, which I found in the electrical section of the hardware store. Then, using the ABS/PVC glue I connected the end cap, and then I went pipe-to-pipe with couplers—almost all the way back to the barrel.

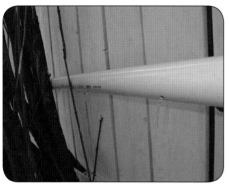

Step 5: Plumb the Barrel

This step proved to be a bit more complicated than I expected, mostly because I was using vacuum tubing/ connectors on one side. However, the only pieces I could find to connect to the barrel were for plumbing. Unfortunately, they were about 1/16 of an inch smaller than I wanted them to be. So after cleaning the inside a bit with a Dremel, I was back in business. I designed this system to be able to store rainwater, but have a spillover pipe that would take any excess into the pipe system and away from the house. This spillover pipe enters the main pipe on the opposite side of the valve (see pictures). I cut holes in the barrel, as I was concerned that the small spigot wouldn't be able to handle any volume of water. I then attached the plumbing fixtures at the top and bottom and used some silicone caulking to seal the connection. I then measured, cut, and glued the pipes, elbows, and valve assembly.

Step 6: Connect the Valve Assembly to the Watering Pipe

This is pretty straight forward—it helps to have a bit of leeway in your watering pipe (the one you drilled holes into). Use couplers if needed and the ABS/PVC glue.

Step 7: Connect to Your Eaves Trough

I did this step a day after I did the other steps, and from one day to the next I learned that the 2" pipe capacity was just barely enough to handle any real volume of water coming from the barrel. So, I opted for a 3" diameter ABS pipe to handle the water coming from the roof. It was a little tricky getting the oversized fixture to attach to my aluminum eave, but with some minor modifications I got it to work. Again, I used some silicone caulking to seal the connection.

Step 8: Test the Connections for Leaks

Finally, if you have a rainstorm, nature will do this for you, but if not (as in my case) I used my garden hose. I learned that I had a small leak coming from the eave connection—which I fixed once it dried out using some more caulking. We haven't had any real rain as of yet, but I anticipate this system working just fine.

rainwater collection and distribution system

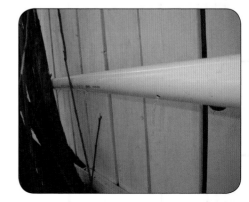

DIY 1000 Watt Wind Turbine

By Steve Spence (sspence)
(www.instructables.com/id/DIY-1000-watt-wind-turbine/)

We built a 1000 watt wind turbine to help charge the battery bank that powers our off-grid home. It's a permanent magnet alternator, generating three-phase AC, rectified to DC, and fed to a charge controller. The magnets spin with the wind and the coils are fixed, so no brushes or slip rings are necessary.

Step 1: Build the Magnet Disks

We had 12" steel disks hydro cut. We cut a template for mounting the magnets. Then we mounted 12-grade n50 magnets around the outside edge. We then built a form, and poured the resin with hardener.

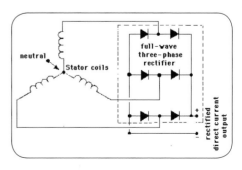

Step 2: Build the Coil Disk

We wound the nine individual coils, soldered them in a three-phase wye configuration, and encased them in resin. We used 35 turns of two parallel strands of 14-gauge enameled (magnet) wire for 12 volts. Use 70 turns of single strand for 24 volts. The three-phase diagram shown here shows three stator coils. Each coil is actually three coils in a series. Coils 1, 4, and 7 are series together, 2, 5, and 8 are series together, and 3, 6, and 9 are series together.

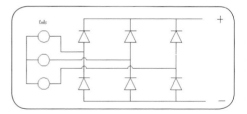

Step 3: Build the Bearing Assembly

Two Harley Davidson wheel bearings are inserted into the pipe, with a smaller pipe locked between them to keep them in place.

Step 4: Construct the Blades

The blades are 2" by 6" pine, cut at 10 degrees on a table saw, and sanded into a rough airfoil. Not perfect, but close enough.

Step 5: Bolt It All Together

How I Built an Electricity-Producing Wind Turbine

By Michael David (mdavis19)
(www.instructables.com/id/How-I-built-an-electricity-producing-wind-turbine/)

Several years ago I bought some remote property in Arizona. I am an astronomer and wanted a place to practice my hobby far away from the terrible light pollution found near cities of any real size. I found a great piece of property. The problem is, it's so remote that there is no electrical service available. That's not really a problem. No electricity equals no light pollution. However, it would be nice to have at least a little electricity, since so much of life in the twenty-first century is dependent on it.

One thing I noticed right away about my property is that most of the time, the wind is blowing. Almost from the moment I bought it, I had the idea of putting up a wind turbine and making

some electricity, and later adding some solar panels. This is the story of how I did it. Not with an expensive, store-bought turbine, but with a home-built one that cost hardly anything. If you have some fabricating skills and some electronic know-how, you can build one too.

Step 1: Acquiring a Generator

I started by Googling for information on home-built wind turbines. There are a lot of them out there in an amazing variety of designs and complexities. All of them had five things in common though:

1. A generator
2. Blades
3. A mounting that keeps it turned into the wind
4. A tower to get it up into the wind
5. Batteries and an electronic control system

I reduced the project to just five little systems. If attacked one at a time, the project didn't seem too terribly difficult. I decided to start with the generator. My online research showed that a lot of people were building their own generators. That seemed a bit too complicated, at least for a first effort. Others were using surplus permanent magnet DC motors as generators in their projects. This looked like a simpler way to go. So I began looking into what motors were best for the job. A lot of people seemed to like to use old computer tape drive motors (surplus relics from the days when computers had big reel to reel tape drives). The best apparently are a couple of models of motor made by Ametek. The best motor made by Ametek is a 99 volt DC motor that works great as a generator. Unfortunately, they are almost impossible to locate these days. There are a lot of other Ametek motors around though. A couple of their other models make decent generators and can still be found on places like eBay. I managed to score one of the good 30 volt Ametek motors off of eBay for only $26. They don't go that cheap these days. People are catching on to the fact that they make great wind generators. Other brands will work, so don't fret about the price Ameteks are going for. Shop wisely. Anyway, the motor I got was in good shape and worked great. Even just giving the shaft a quick turn with my fingers would light a 12 volt bulb quite brightly. I gave it a real test by chucking it up in my drill press and connecting it to a dummy load. It works great as a generator, putting out easily a couple hundred watts with this setup. I knew then that if I could make a decent set of blades to drive it, it would produce plenty of power.

me. I followed that general recipe. I did things a little differently though. I used black ABS pipe since my local home center store just happened to have pre-cut lengths of it. I used 6" pipe instead of 4" pipe and 24 inches instead of 19 5/8. I started by quartering a 24-inch piece of pipe around its circumference and cutting it lengthwise into four pieces. Then I cut out one blade, and used it as a template for cutting out the others. That left me with four blades (three plus one spare). I then did a little extra smoothing and shaping using my belt sander and palm sander on the cut edges to try to make them into better airfoils. I don't know if it's really much of an improvement, but it didn't seem to hurt, and the blades look really good (if I do say so myself).

Step 2: Making the Blades

Blades and a hub to connect them to were the next order of business. More online research ensued. A lot of people made their own blades by carving them out of wood. That looked like an outrageous amount of work to me. I found that other people were making blades by cutting sections out of PVC pipe and shaping them into airfoils. That looked a lot more promising to

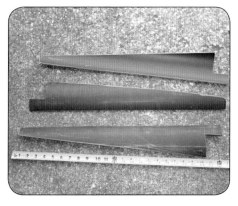

Step 3: Building the Hub

Next I needed a hub to bolt the blades to and attach to the motor. Rummaging around in my workshop, I found a toothed pulley that fit on the motor shaft, but was a little too small in diameter to bolt the blades onto. I also found a scrap disk of aluminum 5 inches in diameter and 1/4" thick that I could bolt the blades onto, but wouldn't attach to the motor shaft. The simple solution of course was to bolt these two pieces together to make the hub. Much drilling, tapping, and bolting later, I had a hub.

Step 4: Building the Turbine Mounting

Next I needed a mounting for the turbine. Keeping it simple, I opted to just strap the motor to a piece of 2 × 4 wood. The correct length of the wood was computed by the highly scientific method of picking the best looking piece of scrap 2 × 4 off my scrap wood pile and going with however long it was. I also cut a piece of 4" diameter PVC pipe to make a shield to go over the motor and protect it from the weather. For a tail to keep it turned into the wind, I again just used a piece of heavy sheet aluminum I happened to have laying around. I was worried that it wouldn't be a big enough tail, but it seems to work just fine. The turbine snaps right around into the wind every time it changes direction. I have

added a few dimensions to the picture. I doubt any of these measurements are critical though. Next, I had to begin thinking about some sort of tower and some sort of bearing that would allow the head to freely turn into the wind. I spent a lot of time in my local home center stores (Lowes and Home Depot) brainstorming. Finally, I came up with a solution that seems to work well. While brainstorming, I noticed that 1" diameter iron pipe is a good slip-fit inside 1 1/4" diameter steel EMT electrical conduit. I could use a long piece of 1 1/4" conduit as my tower and 1" pipe fittings at either end. For the head unit I attached a 1" iron floor flange centered 7 ½ inches back from the generator end of the 2 × 4, and screwed a 10"-long iron pipe nipple into it. The nipple would slip into the top of the piece of conduit I'd use as a tower and form a nice bearing. Wires from the generator would pass through a hole drilled in the 2 × 4 down the center of the pipe/conduit unit and exit at the base of the tower.

Step 5: Build the Tower Base

For the tower base, I started by cutting a 2' diameter disk out of plywood. I made a U-shaped assembly out of 1" pipe fittings. In the middle of that assembly I put a 1 1/4" tee. The tee is free to turn around the 1" pipe and forms a hinge that allows me to raise and lower the tower. I then added a close nipple, a 1 ¼ to 1 reducing fitting, and a 12" nipple. Later I added a 1" tee between the reducer and the 12" nipple so there would be a place for the wires to exit the pipe. This is shown in a photo further down the page. I also later drilled holes in the wooden disk to allow me to use steel stakes to lock it in place on the ground. The second photo shows the head and base together. You can begin to see how it will go together. Imagine a 10' piece of steel conduit connecting the two pieces. Since I was building this thing in Florida, but was going to use it in Arizona, I decided to hold off on purchasing the 10' piece of conduit until I got to Arizona. That meant the wind turbine would not be fully assembled and would not get properly tested until I was ready to put it up in the field. That was a little scary because I wouldn't know if the thing actually worked until I tried it in Arizona.

Step 7: The Finished Head of the Wind Turbine

This photo shows the finished head unit with the blades attached. Is that a thing of beauty or what? It almost looks like I know what I'm doing. I never got a chance to properly test the unit before heading to Arizona. One windy day though, I did take the head outside and hold it high up in the air above my head into the wind just to see if the blades would spin as well as I had hoped. Spin they did. In a matter of a few seconds, the blades spun up to a truly scary speed (no load on the generator), and I found myself holding onto a giant, spinning, whirligig of death, with no idea how to put it down without getting myself chopped to bits. Fortunately, I did eventually manage to turn it out of the wind and slow it down to a non-lethal speed. I won't make that mistake again.

Step 6: Paint All the Wooden Parts

Next, I painted all the wooden parts with a couple of coats of white latex paint I had leftover from another project. I wanted to protect the wood from the weather. This photo also shows the lead counterweight I added to the left side of the 2 × 4 under the tail to balance the head.

Step 8: Build the Charge Controller

Now that I had all the mechanical parts sorted out, it was time to turn toward the electronic end of the project. A wind power system consists of the wind turbine, one or more batteries to store power produced by the turbine, a blocking diode to prevent power from the batteries being wasted spinning the motor/generator, a secondary load to dump power from the turbine into when

the batteries are fully charged, and a charge controller to run everything. There are lots of controllers for solar and wind power systems. Anyplace that sells alternative energy stuff will have them. There are also always a lot of them for sale on eBay. I decided to try building my own though. So it was back to Googling for information on wind turbine charge controllers. I found a lot of information, including some complete schematics, which was quite nice and made building my own unit very easy. Again, while I followed a general recipe from an online source, I did do some things differently. Being an avid electronics tinkerer from an early age, I have a huge stock of electronic components already on hand, so I had to buy very little to complete the controller. I substituted different components for some parts and reworked the circuit a little just so I could use parts I already had on hand. That way I had to buy almost nothing to build the controller. The only part I had to buy was the relay. I built my prototype charge controller by bolting all the pieces to a piece of plywood, as seen in the first photo below. I would rebuild it in a weatherproof enclosure later. Whether you build your own or buy one, you will need some sort of controller for your wind turbine. The general principal behind the controller is that it monitors the voltage of the battery(s) in your system, and either sends power from the turbine into the batteries to recharge them or dumps the power from the turbine into a secondary load if the batteries are fully charged (to prevent over-charging and destroying the batteries). In operation, the wind turbine is connected to the controller. Lines then run from the controller to the battery. All loads are taken directly from the battery. If the battery voltage drops below 11.9 volts, the controller switches the turbine power to charging the

battery. If the battery voltage rises to 14 volts, the controller switches to dumping the turbine power into the dummy load. There are trimpots to adjust the voltage levels at which the controller toggles back and forth between the two states. I chose 11.9V for the discharge point and 14V for the fully charged point based on advice from different web sites on the subject of properly charging lead acid batteries. The sites all recommended slightly different voltages. I sort of averaged them and came up with my numbers. When the battery voltage is between 11.9V and 14.8V, the system can be switched between either charging or dumping. A pair of push buttons allow me to switch between states anytime, for testing purposes. Normally the system runs automatically. When charging the battery, the yellow LED is lit. When the battery is charged and power is being dumped to the dummy load, the green LED is lit. This gives me some minimal feedback on what is going on with the system. I also use my multimeter to measure both battery voltage and turbine output voltage. I will probably eventually add either panel meters or automotive-style voltage and charge/discharge meters to the system. I'll do that once I have it in some sort of enclosure. I used my variable voltage bench power supply to simulate a battery in various states of charge and discharge to test and tune the controller. I could set the voltage of the power supply to 11.9V and set the trimpot for the low voltage trip point. Then I could crank the voltage up to 14V and set the trimpot for the high voltage trimpot. I had to get it set before I took it into the field because I'd have no way to tune it up out there. I have found out the hard way that it is important with this controller design to connect the battery first, and then connect the wind turbine and/or solar panels. If you connect the wind turbine first, the wild voltage swings coming from the turbine won't be smoothed out by the load of the battery, the controller will behave erratically, the relay will click away wildly, and voltage spikes could destroy the ICs. So always connect to the battery(s) first, and then connect the wind turbine. Also, make sure you disconnect the wind turbine first when taking the system apart. Disconnect the battery(s) last.

Step 9: Erect the Tower

At last, all parts of the project were complete. It was all done only a week before my vacation arrived. That was cutting it close. I disassembled the turbine and carefully packed the parts and the tools I'd need to assemble it for their trip across the country. Then I once again I drove out to my remote property in Arizona for a week of off-grid relaxation, but this time with hopes of having some actual electricity on the site. The first order of business was setting up and bracing the tower. After arriving at my property and unloading my van, I drove to the nearest Home Depot (about 60 miles one way) and bought the 10' piece of 1 1/4" conduit I needed for the tower. Once I had it, assembly went quickly. I used nylon rope to anchor the pole to four big wooden stakes driven in the ground. Turnbuckles on the lower

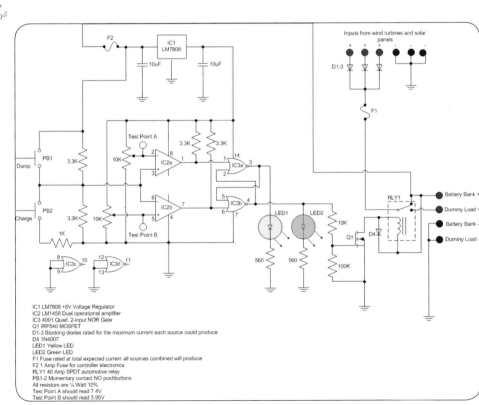

IC1 LM7808 +8V Voltage Regulator
IC2 LM1458 Dual operational amplifier
IC3 4001 Quad. 2-input NOR Gate
Q1 IRF540 MOSFET
D1-3 Blocking diodes rated for the maximum current each source could produce
D4 1N4007
LED1 Yellow LED
LED2 Green LED
F1 Fuse rated at total expected current all sources combined will produce
F2 1 Amp Fuse for controller electronics
RLY1 40 Amp SPDT automotive relay
PB1-2 Momentary contact NO pushbuttons
All resistors are ¼ Watt 10%
Test Point A should read 7.4V
Test Point B should read 5.95V

ends of each guy-line allowed me to plumb up the tower. By releasing the line from either stake in line with the hinge at the base, I could raise and lower the tower easily. Eventually the nylon line and wooden stakes will be replaced with steel stakes and steel cables. For testing though, this arrangement worked fine. The second photo shows a close-up of how the guy-lines attach near the top of the tower. I used chain-link fence brackets as tie points for my guy-lines. The fence brackets don't quite clamp down tightly on the conduit, which is smaller in diameter than the fence posts they are normally used with. So there is a steel hose clamp at either end of the stack of brackets to keep them in place. The third photo shows the base of the tower, staked to the ground, with the wire from the wind turbine exiting from the tee below the conduit tower. I used an old orange extension cord with a broken plug to connect between the turbine and the controller. I simply cut both ends off and put on spade lugs. Threading the wire through the tower turned out to be easy. It was a cold morning and the cord was very stiff. I was able to just push it through the length of the conduit tower. On a warmer day I probably would have had to use a fish tape or string line to pull the cord through the conduit. I got lucky.

Step 10: Erect the Wind Turbine

The first photo shows the turbine head installed on top of the tower. I greased up the pipe on the bottom of the head and slid it into the top of the conduit. It made a great bearing, just as I'd planned. Sometimes I even amaze myself. Too bad there was nobody around to get an Iwo Jima Flag Raising-type picture of me raising the tower up with the head installed. The second photo shows the wind turbine fully assembled. Now I'm just waiting for the wind to blow. Wouldn't you know it, it was dead calm that morning. It was the first calm day I had ever seen out there. The wind had always been blowing every other time I had been there.

Step 11: Connect the Electronics

The first photo below shows the electronics setup. The battery, inverter, meter, and prototype charge controller are all sitting on a plywood board on top of a blue plastic tub. I plug a long extension cord into the inverter and run power back to my campsite. Once the wind starts blowing, the turbine head snaps around into it and begins spinning up. It spins up quickly until the output voltage exceeds the battery voltage plus the blocking diode drop (around 13.2 volts, depending on the state of the battery charge). It is really running without a load until that point. Once that voltage is exceeded, the turbine suddenly has a load as it begins dumping power into the battery. Once under load, the RPMs only slightly increase as the wind speed increases. More wind means more current into the battery which means more load on the generator. So the system is pretty much self-governing. I saw no signs of over-revving. Of course, in storm-force winds, all bets are off. Switching the controller to dump power into the dummy load did a good job of braking the turbine and slowing it way down even in stronger gusts. Actually shorting the turbine output is an even better brake. It brings the turbine to a halt even in strong winds. Shorting the output is how I made the turbine safe to raise and lower, so I wouldn't get sliced and diced by the spinning blades. Warning though, the whole head assembly can still swing around and crack you hard on the noggin if the wind changes direction while you are working on these things. So be careful out there.

Step 12: Enjoy Having Power in the Middle of Nowhere

How sweet it is! I have electricity! Here I have my laptop computer set up and plugged into the power provided by the inverter, which in turn is powered by the wind turbine. I normally only have about two hours of battery life on my laptop. So I don't get to use it much while I'm camping. It comes in handy though for downloading photos out of my camera when its memory card gets full, making notes on projects like this one, working on the next great American novel, or just watching DVD movies. Now I have no battery life problems, at least as long as the wind blows. Besides the laptop, I can also now recharge all my other battery powered equipment like my cell phone, my camera, my electric shaver, my air mattress pump, etc. Life used to get real primitive on previous camping trips when the batteries in all my electronic stuff ran down. I used the wind turbine to power my new popup trailer on a later vacation. The strong spring winds kept the wind turbine spinning all day every day and most of the nights too while I was in Arizona. The turbine provided enough power for the interior 12V lighting and enough for 120V AC at the power outlets to keep my battery charger, electric shaver, and mini vacuum cleaner (camping is messy) all charged up and running. My girlfriend complained about it not having enough power to run her hairdryer though.

Step 13: How Much Did It Cost?

So how much did all this cost to build? Well, I saved all the receipts for everything I bought related to this project.

Part	Origin	Cost
Motor/ generator	eBay	$26.00
Misc. pipe fittings	Homecenter Store	$41.49
Pipe for blades	Homecenter Store	$12.84
Misc hardware	Homecenter Store	$8.00
Conduit	Homecenter Store	$19.95
Wood and aluminum	Scrap Pile	$0.00
Power cable	Old extension cord	$0.00
Rope and turnbuckles	Homecenter Store	$18.47
Electronic parts	Already on hand	$0.00
Relay	Auto Parts Store	$13.87
Battery	Borrowed from my UPS	$0.00
Inverter	Already on hand	$0.00
Paint	Already on hand	$0.00
Total		$140.62

Not too bad. I doubt I could buy a commercially made turbine with a comparable power output, plus a commercially made charge controller, plus a commercially made tower for less than $750-$1000.

added a built in voltage meter. Both were bought cheap on eBay. I have also added a few new features. The unit now has provisions for power inputs from multiple sources. It also has built-in fused 12V power distribution for three external loads.

The second photo shows the inside of the charge controller. I basically just transferred everything that I originally had bolted onto the plywood board in the prototype into this box. I added an automotive illuminated voltage gauge and fuses for three external 12V loads. I used heavy gauge wire to try to reduce losses due to wire resistance. Every watt counts when you are living off-grid.

The third image is the schematic for the new charge controller. It is pretty much the same as the old one above, except for the addition of the volt meter and extra fuse blocks for the external loads.

The photo directly below is a block diagram of the whole power system.

Step 14: Extras

I have completed the rebuild of the charge controller. It is now in a semi-weatherproof enclosure, and I have also

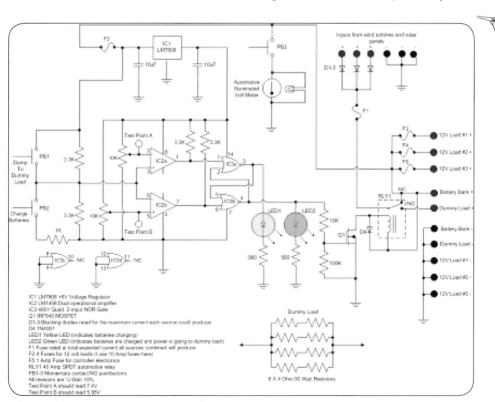

Note that I only have one solar panel built right now. I just haven't had the time to complete the second one.

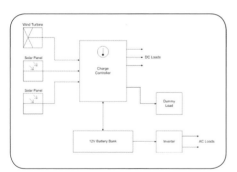

The second photo shows the new charge controller unit. The wires on the left side are coming from the wind turbine and solar panel. The wires on the right side are going to the battery bank and dummy load. I cut up an old heavy-duty 100' extension cord to make cables to connect wind turbine and solar panel to the charge controller. The cable to the wind turbine is about 75 feet long and the cable to the solar panel is about 25 feet long. The battery bank I am currently using consists of eleven sealed lead-acid 12V batteries of 8 Amp-Hour capacity connected in parallel. That gives me 88 Amp-Hours of storage capacity, which is plenty for camping. As long as it is sunny and windy, (nearly every day is sunny and windy on my property), the wind turbine and solar panel keep the batteries well charged.

Step 15: More Extras

Once again I stayed on my remote property during my recent vacation in Arizona. This time I had both my home-built wind turbine and my home-built solar panel with me. Working together, they provided plenty of power for my (admittedly minimal) electricity needs.

Chispito Wind Generator

By velacreations
(www.instructables.com/id/
Chispito-Wind-Generator/)

and empowering than making a wind-powered generator from scrap materials. Most of the tools and materials in this manual can be found in your local hardware shop or junk pile.

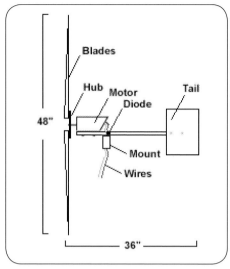

The Chispito Wind Generator was designed to be simple and efficient with fast and easy construction. There are no limits to what you can do with wind power. There is nothing more rewarding

Tools

- drill and drill bits (7/32", ¼", 5/16")
- jigsaw with a metal blade
- pipe
- wrench

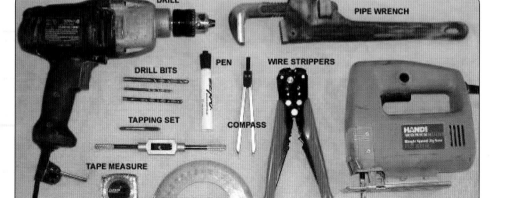

- flat head screwdriver
- crescent wrench
- vise and/or clamp
- wire strippers
- tape measure
- marker
- pen
- compass and protractor
- ¼" #20 Thread Tapping Set
- an extra person helps a lot!

Materials

Buy the hard to find parts at: www. velacreations.com/store.html.

Mount
- 36 inches of 1" square tubing
- 2" floor flange
- 2" by 4" nipple
- (3) 3/4" self-tapping Screws

Note

If you have access to a welder, you can weld a 4" section of 2" pipe onto your square tubing instead of using the flange, nipple, and sheet metal screws.

Motor
- 260 VDC, 5—A continuous duty treadmill motor with a 6" threaded hub

- 30 to 50 amp
- Blocking diode (one-way)
- (20) 5/16" by 1 3/4" motor bolts
- 3" by 11" PVC pipetail
- 1 square foot (approx) lightweight material (metal)
- (2) 3/4" self-tapping screws
- Blades
- 24" length of 8" PVC pipe (if it is UV resistant, you will not need to paint it)
- (6) 1/4"-20 bolts
- (9) 1/4" washers
- 3 sheets A4 paper
- Tape

Step 1: Blades

Cutting Blades—makes nine blades (or three-blade sets) and a thin waste strip.

1. Place the 24" length of PVC pipe and square tubing (or other straight edge) side by side on a flat surface. Push the pipe tight against the tubing and mark the line where they touch. This is Line A.
2. Make a mark near each end of Line A, 23 inches apart.
3. Tape three sheets of A4 paper together, so that they form a long,

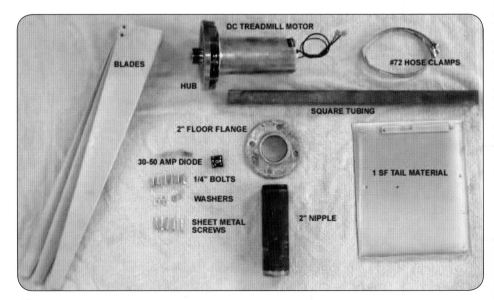

completely straight piece of paper. Wrap this around the section of pipe at each of the two marks you just made, one then the other. Make sure the short side of the paper is straight along Line A and the paper is straight against itself where it overlaps. Mark a line along the edge of the paper at each end. Call one Line B and the other Line C.

4. Start where Line A intersects Line B. Going left around Line B, make a mark at every 145 mm. The last section should be about 115 mm.

5. Start where Line A intersects Line C. Going right around Line C, make a mark at every 145 mm. The last section should be about 115 mm.

6. Mark each line using a straight edge.

7. Cut along these lines, using the jigsaw, so that you have four strips of 145 mm and one strip about 115 mm.

8. Take each strip and place them with the inside of the pipe facing down.

9. Make a mark at one end of each strip 115 mm from the left edge.

10. Make a mark at the other end of each strip 30 mm from the left edge.

11. Mark and cut these lines, using the jigsaw.

12. Place each blade with the inside of the pipe facing down.

13. Make a mark along the angled line of the blade, 3 inches from the wide end.

14. Make another mark on the wide end of the blade, one inch from the straight edge.

15. Connect these two marks and cut along the line. This prevents the blades from interfering with the others' wind.

Sanding the Blades

You should sand the blades to achieve the desired airfoil. This will increase the efficiency of the blades, as well as make them quieter. The angled (leading) edge wants to be rounded, while the straight (tailing) edge wants to be pointed. Any sharp corners should be slightly rounded to cut down on noise.

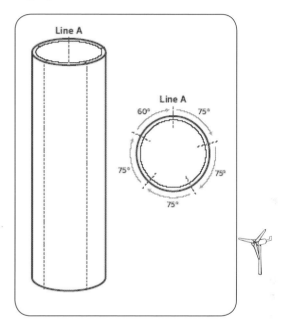

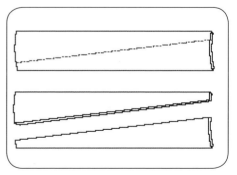

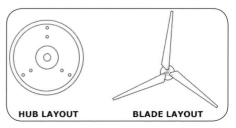

HUB LAYOUT   BLADE LAYOUT

Step 2: Hub and Mount

Cutting Tail

The exact dimensions of the tail are not important. You want about one square foot of lightweight material, preferably metal. You can make the tail any shape you want, so long as the end result is stiff rather than floppy.

Drilling Holes in Square Tubing: Using the 5/16" drill bit

1. Place the motor on the front end of the square tubing, so that the hub part hangs over the edge and the bolt holes of the motor face down.
2. Roll the motor back so you can see the bolt holes, and mark their position on the square tubing.
3. Drill a 5/16" hole at each mark all the way through the square tubing.

Floor Flange Holes

This will be dealt with in the assembly section of this manual, as these holes are what determine the balance.

Drilling Holes in Blades: Using the ¼" drill bit

1. Mark two holes at the wide end and along the straight edge of each of the three blades. The first hole should be 3/8 of an inch from the straight edge and 3/8 of an inch from the bottom. The second hole should be 3/8 of an inch from the straight edge and 1¼ inches from the bottom.

2. Drill these six holes.

Drilling and Tapping Holes in Hub: Using the 7/32" drill bit and ¼" tap

1. The treadmill motor comes with the hub attached. To take it off, hold the end of the shaft (which comes through the hub) firmly with pliers, and turn the hub clockwise. This hub unscrews clockwise, which is why the blades turn counter-clockwise.
2. Make a template of the hub on a piece of paper, using a compass and protractor.
3. Mark three holes, each of which is 2 3/8 inches from the center of the circle and equidistant from each other.
4. Place this template over the hub and punch a starter hole through the paper and onto the hub at each hole.
5. Drill these holes with the 7/32" drill bit.
6. Tap the holes with the ¼" × 20 tap.
7. Bolt the blades onto the hub using the ¼" bolts. At this point, the outer holes have not been drilled.
8. Measure the distance between the straight edge of the tips of each blade. Adjust them so that they are all equidistant. Mark and punch each hole on the hub through the empty hole in each blade.

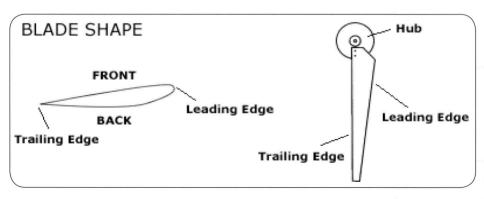

BLADE SHAPE

FRONT

BACK

Leading Edge

Trailing Edge

Hub

Leading Edge

Trailing Edge

9. Label the blades and hub so that you can match which blade goes where at a later stage.

10. Remove the blades and then drill and tap these outer three holes.

Making a Protective Sleeve for the Motor

1. Draw two straight lines, about ¾" apart, along the length of the 3" by 11" PVC pipe. Cut along these lines.

2. Make a 45-degree cut at the end of the pipe.

3. Place needle nose pliers inside the strip that has been cut out, and pry the pipe apart.

4. Making sure the bolt holes of the motor are centered in the middle of the missing strip of PVC pipe, push the motor into the pipe. An extra person will make this a lot easier.

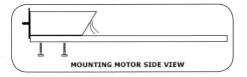

MOUNTING MOTOR SIDE VIEW

Step 3: Assembly

1. Place the motor on top of the square tubing and bolt it in, using the two 5/16" by 1 3/4" bolts.

2. Place the diode on the square tubing, about 2 inches behind the motor, and screw it into position using the self-tapping metal screw.

3. Connect the black wire coming out of the motor to the positive incoming terminal of the diode (labeled AC on the positive side).

4. Connect the red wire coming out of the motor to the negative incoming terminal of the diode (labeled AC on the negative side).

5. Center the tail over the square tubing at the back end. Clamp your tail onto the side of the square tubing.

6. Using two self-tapping screws, screw the tail in place.

7. Place each blade on the hub so that all the holes line up. Using the ¼" bolts and washers, bolt the blades to the hub. For the inner three holes, use two washers per bolt, one on each side of the blade. For the outer three holes, just use one washer next to the head of the bolt. Tighten.

8. Hold the end of the shaft of the motor (which comes through the hub) firmly with pliers, and turn the hub counterclockwise until it tightens and stops.

9. Screw the nipple tightly into the floor flange using a pipe wrench.

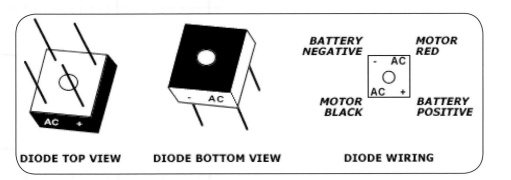

DIODE TOP VIEW   DIODE BOTTOM VIEW   DIODE WIRING

10. Clamp the nipple in a vice so that the floor flange is facing up and level.
11. Place the square tubing (and everything that is on it) on top of the floor flange and move it so that it is perfectly balanced.
12. Through the holes of the floor flange, mark the square tubing at the point of balance.
13. Drill these two holes using a 5/32" drill bit. You will probably have to take off the hub and tail to do this.
14. Attach the square tubing to the floor flange with two sheet metal screws. For a longer life span of your wind generator, you should paint the blades, motor sleeve, mount, and tail.

Step 4: Additional Information
Use of Chispito Wind Generator

You will need a tower, wire, ammeter, charge controller/regulator, and a battery bank for your Chispito Wind Generator.

Tower

The tower is one of the most important components in your wind generator system. It must be strong, stable, easily raised and lowered, and well anchored. The higher your tower is, the more wind your generator will be exposed to. Guy wires must be placed at least every 18 feet of tower height. Guy wires must be anchored to the ground at least 50 percent of the height away from the base.

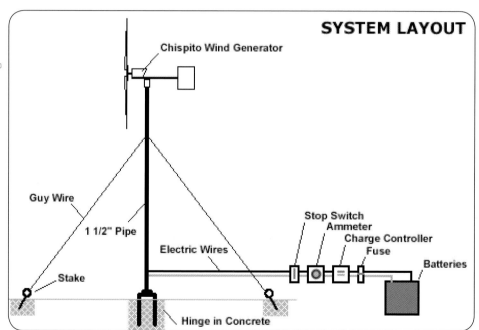

SYSTEM LAYOUT

Chispito Wind Generator

Guy Wire

1 1/2" Pipe

Electric Wires

Stake

Hinge in Concrete

Stop Switch
Ammeter
Charge Controller
Fuse
Batteries

Tools You'll need
- Tin snips
- Soldering iron
- Pliers (with cutters)
- Drill bits
- Sandpaper
- M6 tap for cutting the threads. This is not essential as you could just use an ordinary nut, but it's neater.
- Drill (drill press makes life easier . . .)
- Glue or glue gun

The thermoelectric lamp generates electricity off the temperature difference between the hot candle and the cool heat sink. This we can use to power small devices, like a radio or very bright LEDs. You may be able to charge an MP3 player off of it, too!

Here's What You'll Need
- A thermoelectric peltier chip, the bigger the better; I used a 100W version.
- A large heat sink; I used a dell one with heat pipes. The success depends on this heat sink, so get the best you can!
- An emergency phone charger (we are going to steal the joule thief out of it).
- A small amount of rock wool insulation; small amounts available from garden centers.
- A small tin can with a lip around the top. (Heinz beans will do.)
- A Coke can.
- Thermal heat compound
- Some heavy duty foil, about 30 × 30cm
- A foot of thick copper or steel wire for the handle.
- (2) 25mm long M6 Bolts
- (4) 40mm long M5 Bolts
- (1) 50mm long M5 Bolt
- The bolts don't need to be any exact size, just use whatever is available; almost any will work.

Step 1: Drill the Holes in the Can and Fit the Feet and Central Adjustment

You can see that I have drilled five holes in the bottom of the can. These are for the feet and candle height adjustment. I fitted little rubber feet to them; this is not essential.

Step 2: Tighten Them All Up and Glue the Central Nut in Place

Once you've tightened all of the feet up, you need to glue the central nut in place.

You can see I've added a cardboard shim inside of the can. This because the Coke can is slightly too small for the tin can. The shim prevents it from tipping slightly when the candle height is adjusted. The cardboard only needs to be about 25mm high.

Step 3: Cut the Candle Door

Next you need to cut the hole for the candle in the side of the can; this should be around 30 to 35 mm by about 50 mm long. I started by drilling a small hole and worked from there using the tin snips. After this you can drill the ventilation holes all the way around the top of the can. I used a 3mm drill bit for this.

Make sure you sand all the edges so you can't cut yourself on the metal!

Step 4: Cut the Coke Can to Size

Now cut the Coke can to about half off the height of the tin can. You can see in the photo I am testing the height of the flame; we want it to be around 6mm away from the ruler with a new candle. You'll probably have to make a few adjustments to get this right.

Step 5: Fit Some Rock Wool to the Coke Can

Next turn the Coke can over and fill it with rock wool insulation. Poke a space in the middle with a pen or something similar for the bolt to go into.

Step 6: Test if the Coke Can Fits in the Tin Can

Now you can fit the coke can in place. You can see a little dimple in the middle; this is because the coke can was forced down to give the bolt something to rest on. The coke can might not fit perfectly on the bolt because of the insulation, you might need to wiggle it about a bit. Test the movement to make sure you can adjust the height smoothly.

Step 7: Fit the Handle

Next, you can form the handle for carrying the device. I used some thick copper wire as a handle because it matches the heat sink pipes. You need to bend the handle back through the holes to prevent it from turning (see the photo). This stops the device rotating upside down when you are carrying it (the heat sink is the heaviest part).

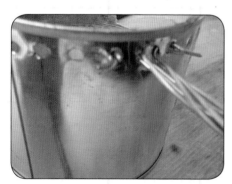

Step 8: Drill the Heat Sink for the Peltier Holder

Now we can work on the heat sink. Here I have drilled two holes to mount the peltier. You can either tap the holes or use a locknut on the other side. The two holes need to be set so that the bolts fit inside of the tin can; this keeps the peltier in the right position. I have

also cleaned the heat sink, so it will be ready for the thermal compound.

Step 9: Cut the Peltier Holder to Size

Next you can make the cover for the peltier. It's easier to cut the square out with this part still attached to the can—cut the square and then use a can opener to remove the bottom. Mark around the peltier with a marker or a scribe and drill a hole in the center. Work out from this using the tin snips to make the square. The square needs to be slightly smaller than the peltier chip so that it grips it. Mark the two holes the same as on the heat sink and drill them for the correct size. I made the cut out slightly round so I wouldn't cut through the strengthening ribs on the tin lid.

Step 10: Apply Thermal Compound

Now you can apply the thermal compound to the heat sink. Make sure it is clean and spread the compound over the contact area. Note: The thermal compound only needs to be a very fine layer, not a thick paste like I have done here. There is a little too much thermal compound in the photo.

Step 11: Fit the Peltier

Now you can fit the peltier to the heat sink. Press it down into the thermal compound and wiggle to smooth out the compound. You can see that the peltier is very dirty from soot, this is from my testing. The side that is in contact with the heat sink must be clean though. When you use the device, try and avoid getting soot on the peltier as it blocks the heat transfer. Use the candle height adjustment to get this right.

Step 12: Insulate the Peltier

Now you need to make a thermal insulator for between the heat sink and the fire tin. Cut a square out of the foil the same size as the peltier chip and fit this over the peltier. Fill around the sides with 5mm thick strips of rock wool. Fold the foil over and you should end up with something like in the picture. Don't

worry if it is too thick, as the bolts will compress it when tightened.

Step 13: Cut an Aluminum Patch for the Peltier

Now cut a square of aluminum the same size as the peltier chip. Sand the patch with fine paper to remove the paint. Apply thermal compound (the same as in step 10) and gently place it over the peltier ready for step 14.

I ended up replacing the steel and aluminum plate with a thick aluminum plate to help keep the temperature steady. See the photos for how I made it.

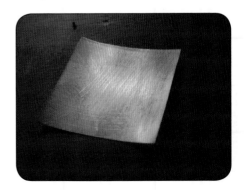

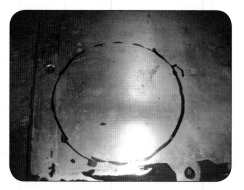

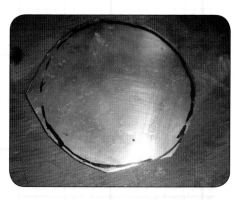

Step 14: Bolt the Peltier Down

Now you can bolt the peltier down. You'll need to punch some holes in the rock wool insulator for the bolts.

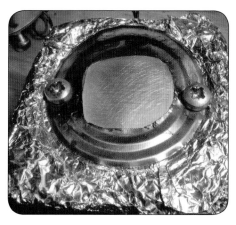

Step 15: Solder and Fit the Joule Thief

You can remove the battery pack from the emergency charger and just use the plastic end cap with the circuit in it.

First check the polarity of the wires to make sure that you know which way to solder them on. You can do this by just trying them both ways to see which way works. Do this with the peltier heated by the candle. You'll need to solder the wires onto the joule thief and attach the joule thief to the tin can. I just used hot melt glue to fix it in place. You should have a nice 2.5mm output jack where you can plug things in.

Step 16: Finished Product

It should be finished now! Try various loads in the output to see what kind of power you get. Different peltiers will put out different amounts of power; it also depends on the temperature difference you manage to achieve. I managed to charge my small MP3 player, but it didn't have enough power to charge my phone. You can see it powering an LED torch here.

Build a 60 Watt Solar Panel

By Michael Davis (mdavid19)
(www.instructables.com/id/
Build-a-60-Watt-
Solar-Panel/)

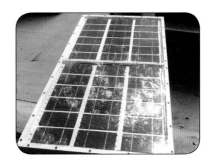

Several years ago I bought some remote property in Arizona. I am an astronomer and wanted a place to practice my hobby far away from the terrible light pollution found near cities of any real size. I found a great piece of property. The problem is, it's so remote that there is no electricity available. That's not really a problem. No electricity equals no light pollution. However, it would be nice to have at least a little electricity, since so much of life in the twenty-first century is dependent on it.

I built a wind turbine to provide some power on the remote property (will be another Instructable in the future). It works great, when the wind blows. However, I wanted more power and more dependable power. The wind seems to blow all the time on my property, except when I really need it to. I do get well over 300 sunny days a year on the property though, so solar power seemed like the obvious choice to supplement the wind turbine. Solar panels are very expensive though. So I decided to try my hand at building my own. I used common tools and inexpensive and easy to acquire materials to build a solar panel that rivals commercial panels in power production, but completely blows them away in price. Read on for step-by-step instructions on how I did it.

Step 1: Buy Some Solar Cells

I bought a couple of bricks of 3 × 6 mono-crystalline solar cells. It takes a total of 36 of these type solar cells wired in series to make a panel. Each cell produces about ½ volt. Thirty-six in a series would give about 18 volts, which would be good for charging 12 volt batteries. (Yes, you really need that high a voltage to effectively charge 12 volt batteries.) This type of solar cell is as thin as paper and as brittle and fragile as glass. They are very easily damaged. The eBay seller of the cells I purchased dipped stacks of 18 in wax to stabilize them and make it easier to ship them without damaging them. The wax is quite a pain to remove though. If you can, find cells for sale that aren't dipped in wax. Keep in mind though that they may suffer some more damage in shipping. Notice that these cells have metal tabs on them. You want cells with tabs on them. You are already going to have to do a lot of soldering to build a panel from tabbed solar cells. If you buy cells without tabs, it will at least double the amount of soldering you have to do. So pay extra for tabbed cells.

I also bought a couple of lots of cells that weren't dipped in wax from another eBay seller. These cells came packed in a plastic box. They rattled around in the box and got a little chipped up on the edges and corners. Minor chips don't really matter too much. They won't reduce the cell's output enough to worry about. These are all blemished and factory seconds anyway. The main reason solar cells get rejected is for chips. So what's another chip or two? All together I bought enough cells to make two panels. I knew I'd probably break or otherwise ruin at least a few during construction, so I bought extras.

Step 2: Build the Box

So what is a solar panel anyway? It is basically a box that holds an array of solar cells. So I started out by building myself a shallow box. I made the box shallow so the sides won't shade the solar cells when the sun comes at an angle. It is made of 3/8"-thick plywood with 3/4 × 3/4 pieces of wood around the edges. The pieces are glued and screwed in place. This panel will hold 36 3 × 6 inch solar cells. I decided to make two sub-panels of 18 cells each just so make it easier to assemble. I knew I would be working at my kitchen table when I would be soldering the cells together, and would have limited work space. So there is a center divider

across the middle of the box. Each sub-panel will fit into one well in the main panel. The second photo is my sort of back of the envelope sketch showing the overall dimensions of the solar panel. All dimensions are in inches (sorry you fans of the metric system). The side pieces are 3/4 by 3/4 and go all the way around the edges of the plywood substrate. Also a piece goes across the center to divide the panel into two sub-panels. This is just the way I chose to do it. There is nothing critical about these dimensions, or even the overall design.

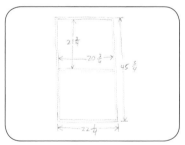

Step 3: Finishing the Box

Here is a close-up showing one half of the main panel. This well will hold one 18-cell sub-panel. Notice the little holes drilled in the edges of the well. This will be the bottom of the panel (it is upside down in the photo). These are vent holes to keep the air pressure inside the panel equalized with the outside, and to let moisture escape. These holes must be on the bottom of the panel or rain and dew will run inside. There must also be vent holes in the center divider between the two sub panels. After using the panel for a while, I now recommend that the vent holes be increased to at least ¼" in diameter. Also, to keep dust and critters out of the panel, stuff a little fiberglass insulation in the holes in the bottom rail of the panel. The insulation is not needed in the holes in the center divider.

Next I cut two pieces of Masonite peg board to fit inside the wells. These pieces of pegboard will be the substrates that each sub-panel will be built on. They were cut to be a loose fit in the wells. You don't have to use peg board for this. I just happened to have some on hand. Just about any thin, rigid and non-conducting material should work. To protect the solar cells from the weather, the panel will have a Plexiglas front. In the third picture, two pieces of scrap Plexiglas have been cut to fit the front of the panel. I didn't have one piece big enough to do the whole thing. Glass could also be used for this, but glass is fragile. Hail stones and flying debris that would shatter glass will just bounce off the Plexi. Now you can start to see what the finished panel will look like.

Step 4: Paint the Box

Next I gave all the wooden parts of the panel several coats of paint to protect them from moisture and the weather. The box was painted inside and out. The type of paint and color was scientifically chosen by shaking all the paint cans I had laying around in my garage and choosing the one that felt like it had enough left in it to do the whole job. The peg board pieces were also painted. They got several coats on both sides. Be sure to paint them on both sides or they will warp when exposed to moisture. Warping could damage the solar cells that will be glued to them.

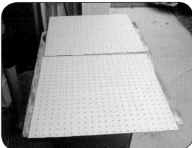

Step 5: Prepare the Solar Cells

Now that I had the structure of the panel finished, it was time to get the solar cells ready. As I said above, getting the wax off the cells is a real pain. After some trial and error, I came up with a way that works fairly well. Still, I would recommend buying from someone who doesn't dip their cells in wax. This photo shows the complete setup I used. My girlfriend asked what I was cooking. Imagine her surprise when I said solar cells. The initial hot water bath for melting the wax is in the right-rear. On the left-front is a bath of hot soapy water. On the right-front is a bath of hot clean water. All the pots are at just below boiling temperature. The sequence I used was to melt the bricks apart in the hot water bath on the right-rear. I'd tease the cells apart and transfer them one at a time to the soapy water bath on the left-front to remove any wax on the cell. Then the cell would be given a rinse in the hot clean water on the right-front. The cells would then be set out to dry on a towel. You should change the water frequently in the soapy and rinse water baths. Don't pour the water down the sink though, because the wax will solidify in your drains and clog them up. Dump the water outside. This process removed almost all the wax from the cells. There is still a very light film on some of the cells, but it doesn't seem to interfere with soldering or the working of the cells. Don't let the water boil in any of the pans or the bubbles will jostle the cells against each other violently. Also, boiling water may be hot enough to loosen the electrical connections on the cells. I also recommend putting the brick of cells in the water cold, and then slowly heating it up to just below boiling temperature to avoid harsh thermal shocks to the cells. Plastic tongs and spatulas come in handy for teasing the

cells apart once the wax melts. Try not to pull too hard on the metal tabs or they may rip off. I found that out the hard way while trying to separate the cells. Good thing I bought extras.

Step 6: Solder the Solar Cells Together

I started out by drawing a grid pattern on each of the two pieces of pegboard, lightly in pencil, so I would know where each of the 18 cells would be located. Then I laid out the cells on that grid pattern upside-down so I could solder them together. All 18 cells on each half panel need to be soldered together in series, and then both half panels need to be connected in series to get the desired voltage. Soldering the cells together was tricky at first, but I got the hang of it fairly quickly. Start out with just two cells upside-down. Lay the solder tabs from the front of one cell across the solder points on the back of the other cell. I made sure the spacing between the cells matched the grid pattern. I continued this until I had a line of six cells soldered together. I then soldered tabs from scrapped solar cells to the solder points on the last cell in the string. Then I made two more lines of six cells. I used a low-wattage soldering iron and fine rosin-core solder. I also used a rosin pen on the solder points on the back of the cells before soldering. Use a really light touch with the soldering iron. The cells are thin and delicate. If you push too hard, you will break the cells. I got careless a couple of times and had to scrap a couple of cells.

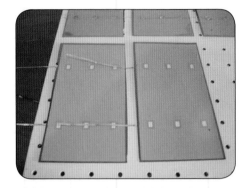

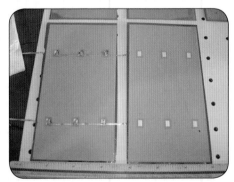

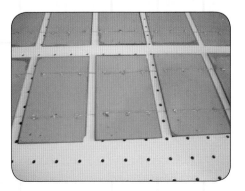

Step 7: Glue Down the Solar Cells

Gluing the cells in place proved to be a little tricky. I placed a small blob of clear silicone caulk in the center of each cell in a six-cell string. Then I flipped the string over and set in place on the pencil line grid I had laid out earlier. I pressed lightly in the center of each cell to get it to stick to the pegboard panel. Flipping the floppy string of cells is tricky. Another set of hands may be useful in during this step. Don't use too much glue, and don't glue the cells anywhere but at their centers. The cells and the panel they are mounted on will expand, contract, flex, and warp with changes in temperature and humidity. If you glue the cells too tightly to the substrate, they will crack in time. Gluing them at only one point in the center allows the cells to float freely on top of the substrate. Both can expand and flex more or less independently, and the delicate solar cells won't crack. Next time I will do it differently. I will solder tabs onto the backs of all the solar cells. Then I will glue all the cells down in their proper places. Then I will solder the tabs together. It seems like the obvious way to go to me now, but I had to do it the hard way once to figure it out. Here is one half panel, finally finished.

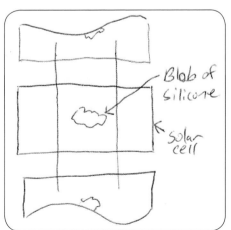

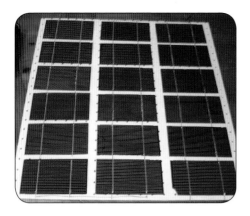

Step 8: Interconnect the Strings of Solar Cells and Test the Half Panel

Here I used copper braid to interconnect first and second strings of cells. You could use solar cell tabbing material or even regular wire. I just happened to have the braid on hand. There is another similar interconnection between the second and third strings at the opposite end of the board. I used blobs of silicone caulk to anchor the braid and prevent it from flopping around. The second photo shows a test of the first half panel outside in the sun. In weak sun through clouds the half panel is producing 9.31 volts. It works! Now all I had to do is build another one just like it. Once I had two half panels complete, I installed them in their places in the main panel frame and wired them together.

Step 9: Install the Half Panels in the Box

Each of the half panels dropped right into their places in the main panel frame. I used four small screws (like the silver one in the photo) to anchor each of the half panels in place.

Step 10: Interconnect the Two Half Panels

Wires to connect the two half panels together were run through the vent holes in the central divider. Again, blobs of silicone caulk were used to anchor the wire in place and prevent it from flopping around.

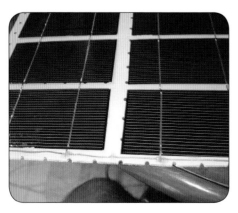

Step 11: Install the Blocking Diode

Each solar panel in a solar power system needs a blocking diode in series with it to prevent the panel from discharging your batteries at night or during cloudy weather. I used a Schottky diode with a 3.3 amp current rating. Schottky diodes have a much lower forward voltage drop than ordinary rectifier diodes, so less power is wasted. Every watt counts when you are off-grid. I got a package of 25 31DQ03 Schottky diodes on eBay for only a few bucks. So I have enough leftovers for lots more solar panels

My original plan was to mount the diode in line with the positive wire outside the panel. After looking at the spec-sheet for the diode though, I decided to mount it inside since the forward voltage drop gets lower as the temperature rises. It will be warmer inside the panel and the diode will work more efficiently. More silicone caulk was used to anchor the diode and wires.

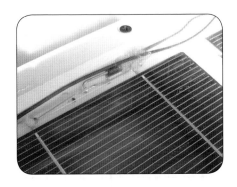

Step 12: Run Wires Outside and Put on the Plexiglas Covers

I drilled a hole in the back of the panel near the top for the wires to exit. I put a knot in the wires for strain relief and anchored them in place with yet more of the silicone caulk.

It is important to let all the silicone caulk cure well before screwing the Plexiglas covers in place. I have found through past experience that the fumes from the caulk may leave a film on the inside of the Plexiglas and on the cells if it isn't allowed to thoroughly cure in the open air before you screw on the covers.

And still more silicone caulk was used to seal the outside of the panel where the wires exit.

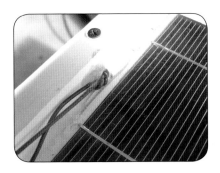

Step 13: Add a Plug

I added a polarized two-pin Jones plug to the end of the panel wires. A mating female plug will be wired into the charge controller I use with my home-built wind turbine so the solar panel can supplement its power production and battery-charging capacity.

Step 14: The Completed Panel

Here is the completed panel with the Plexiglas covers screwed into place. It isn't sealed shut yet at this point. I wanted to wait until after testing it because was worried that I might have to get back inside it if there were problems. Sure enough, a tab popped off one of the cells. Maybe it was due to thermal stresses or shock from handling. Who knows? I opened up the panel and replaced that one cell. I haven't had any more trouble since. I will probably seal the panel with either a bead of silicone caulk, or aluminum AC duct tape wrapped around the edges.

Step 15: Testing the Solar Panel

The first photo shows the voltage output of the completed panel in bright winter sunlight. My meter says 18.88 volts with no load. That's exactly what I was aiming for. In the second photo I am testing the current capacity of the panel, again in bright winter sunlight. My meter says 3.05 amps short circuit current. That is right about what the cells are rated for. So the panel is working very well.

Step 16: Using the Solar Panel

Here is a photo of the solar panel in action, providing much needed power on my remote Arizona property. I used an old extension cord to bring the power from the panel located in a sunny clearing over to my campsite under the trees. I cut the original ends off the cord and installed Jones plugs. You could stick with the original 120V connectors, but I wanted to make sure there was absolutely no chance of accidentally plugging the low-voltage DC equipment into 120V AC. I have to move the panel several times each day to keep it pointed at the sun, but that isn't really a big hardship. Maybe someday I will build a tracking system to automatically keep it aimed at the sun.

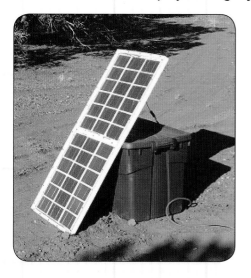

sorts of building supplies and hardware. I also have a lot of useful scrap pieces of wood, wire, and all sorts of miscellaneous stuff (some would say junk) laying around the shop. So I had a lot of stuff on hand already. Your mileage may vary.

Part:	Origin:	Cost:
Solar cells	eBay	$74.00*
Misc. lumber	Home Center Store	$20.62
Plexiglas	Scrap Pile	$0.00
Screws and misc. hardware	Already on hand	$0.00
Silicone caulk	Home Center Store	$3.95
Wire	Already on hand	$0.00
Diode	eBay	$0.20+
Jones plug	Newark Electronics	$6.08
Paint	Already on hand	$0.00

Total: $104.85

Not too bad! That's a fraction of what a commercially made solar panel with a comparable power output would cost, and it was easy. I already have plans to build more panels to add to the capacity of my system.

I actually bought four lots of 18 solar cells on eBay. This price represents only the two lots that went into building this panel. Also, the price of factory second solar cells on eBay has gone up quite a lot recently as oil prices have skyrocketed.

This price represents one out of a lot of 25 diodes I bought on eBay for $5.00.

Step 17: Counting the Cost

So how much did all this cost to build? Well, I saved all the receipts for everything I bought related to this project. Also, my workshop is well stocked with all

Solar Power System

By Mr. Chicken
(www.instructables.com/id/Solar-Power-System/)

This Instructable will show you everything you need to put together a pretty good sized electric solar panel system.

Things you will need:
Supplies
- solar panels
- charge controller
- battery charger
- 2 AWG cable
- at least one 12 volt marine deep cycle battery
- mechanical lugs
- 1 power inverter
- 1 Rubbermaid tote or other container
- 1 battery charger

Tools
- cable cutters
- red electrical tape
- screwdriver
- drill
- crescent wrench

Gather supplies and let's get started.

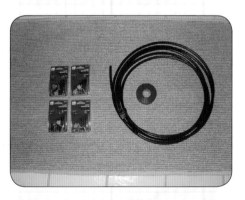

Step 1: Preparing the Batteries

The first thing you want to do is charge your batteries with a charger. This will insure they are charged to capacity and ready to go at set up. I purchased my batteries new and they were only at about 60 percent. While the batteries are charging, you can set up the solar panels and get them wired up and ready to go.

amps. If you want to run say, a 2400 watt inverter, you should use two cables per jumper. Measure between terminals and cut the cable to length. Then add the mechanical lugs. Since the battery terminals were a bit bigger than the holes in the lugs I bought, I drilled them out to fit.

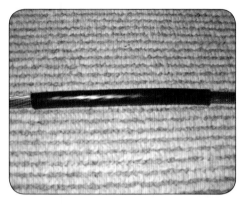

Step 2: Place Batteries in Container

Once the batteries are fully charged, place them in the container and make sure all the positive (+) terminals are on one side and negative (-) on the other. Once in place, measure from terminal to terminal to make the jumpers.

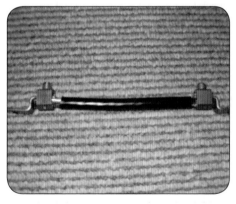

Step 3: Creating the Jumpers

Next, we want to connect the batteries in parallel. To do this, make some jumpers out of 2 AWG cable. Note: Make sure to size your jumpers for your system. If you want to use a larger inverter you will need to use a larger cable. 1200 watts/12 volts 5100 amps. Depending on where you look, 2 AWG cable is good for around 100

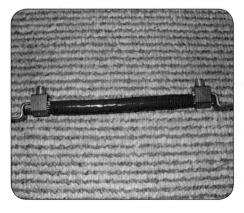

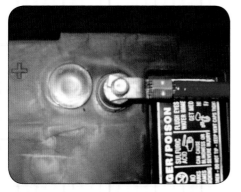

Step 5: Connecting the Charge Controller and Inverter to the Batteries

Next we connect the charge controller and the inverter to the batteries. You will want to make sure the inverter is turned off and the charge controller is not connected to the solar panels yet.

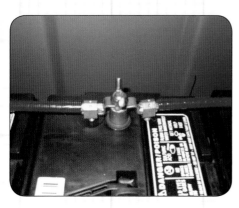

Step 4: Preparing the Lid

Now, add some holes in the lid to run the wires for the charge controller and the inverter. I wanted the charge controller outside so it was visible. You could just as easily put it inside the container for a more concealed look.

Step 6: Final Set Up and Test

It should all be wired together. All that is left is to connect the charge controller to the solar panels and turn the inverter on and check to see that it works.

Step 7: Some Final Thoughts

I originally made this set up as a backup power source for when the power went out. But, I think I will use it more often than that. I don't think the solar panels are powerful enough to charge the batteries after depleting them every day. I will use it for a few days and update how well the system charges with constant use. I originally tested out a single battery and was able to run a lamp and my laptop for about five hours before I finally shut it off. The good thing about this inverter is it will shut off automatically if the voltage drops too low to prevent depleting the batteries. I'm pretty confident that with the three batteries I will be able to power larger items for an extended period of time. Also, this is a pretty expensive set up, about $650.

My costs (without tax or shipping charges) and where I got things:

- Solar panels—$250 (used from craigslist)
- Marine batteries—$240 (for three from Wal-Mart)
- 2 AWG Cables—$5 (for about 2 feet from Lowe's)
- Lugs—$8 (for eight from Lowe's)
- 1200 W inverter—$130 (Amazon. com)
- I had the Rubbermaid container and battery charger, and the charge controller came with the solar panels.

I don't think it unrealistic to spend around $700 or so, possibly more depending on how you set your system up. Depending on how this works I will most likely upgrade to some better solar panels, increase the solar panel array size, and get some more batteries.

This is not "How to Make PV Solar *Cells*". It is possible to home-make Copper Oxide and other kinds of materials, but that is a whole other story, which I may do in the future. It might be a little ambitious to explain how I made PV solar panels out of various types of cells, how and where I obtained those cells inexpensively, the differences in various kinds of cells, and how to work with them to get free electricity from the sun and other sources of light. In essence, this involves ways to connect cells, which may produce more or less than one volt. Also, you are not only trying to increase power output but also decrease the load; that is, efficiently conserve the energy whether it is meager or significant. For example, even the weakest solar panels can run watches, calculators, and radios, charge batteries, and, if it were specifically designed to, power a computer as it would a calculator. Here are some pictures of Solar Panels that I have constructed.

Supplies and Sources

What you may be able to use to build a useful solar panel:

- "Broken" solar cells. They are very cheap and they work, they are just randomly shaped. They are usually crystalline silicon ones, which *always* look broken even when they are not.
- Surplus solar cells: Amorphous silicon printed on glass are excellent, usually producing more than a volt, and much sturdier than the thin ones that break in bulk quantities. If these break, they usually can be fixed.

- Indium Copper Selenide Cells: These are "new" and are conveniently sold as glass tiles with easy to solder tabs.
- Any of the above, sold as cells prepared for assembly into panels; in other words, complete and solder-ready or with wires and tabs. (I will explain how to prepare inferior quality cells in this Instructable.)
  Miscellaneous items:
- wire glue—There is already another Instructable for using wire glue on broken solar cells.
- brass extrusions bracket |_| shaped—Convenient for connecting to glass cells.
- solder
- soldering iron—low wattage
- small flat-head screwdriver
- thin (around 20 AWG or less) stranded copper wire
- lamp cord or speaker wire
- alligator clips
- deep picture frames or shadow boxes—look for imported frames at the El Cheapo store and pray a machine made them
- acrylic/Lexan/Plexiglas/etc. clear polymer sheets
- router or Dremel to cut out the middle of one out of three sheets
- RTV (Silicone Glue) or high temperature hot melt glue (Caution—you don't want the sun to melt it!)
- Rectifier diode such as 1N4001 or 1N4004
- voltage doubler or multiplier circuits (you can make) to increase voltage output—examples: ICL7660, MAX1044, MAX232, etc.
- wide sticky tape
- double sticky foam tape
- rechargeable nickel batteries
- gel cells or car battery (you have one, might as well use it until it's useless)—Li-Ion are not recommended because they are harder to charge

- analog volt meter (only because it doesn't need batteries like a digital one)
- AC inverter—if you are charging a powerful battery and would occasionally run some main-powered appliances. Some UPSs can be easily modified to be inverters, if they can be turned on after a power failure.
  Sources:
  Broken Solar Cells:
  Herbach and Rademan
  Silicon Solar
  Electronic Goldmine Glass (Amorphous) Solar Cells:
  Electronic Goldmine
  Note: Other stores listed may also supply glass solar cells.
  Indium Copper Selenide Cells.
  All Electronics
  Edmund Scientific
  Electronic Goldmine

Other sources
Cheap weather damaged solar powered outdoor night lights—(common failures are circuit corrosion and defective batteries, not the solar cells). Defective solar calculators, solar charged flashlights, etc.

Perhaps a little off topic
For a reasonably good deal on Complete and Useful Solar Panels I recommend "Solar Car Battery Chargers" that are about one or two watts and between $20 and $30 whenever an opportunity to get some arises. But those are what I am trying to show how to make an approximate equivalent of.

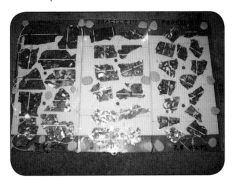

Step 1: How to Use "Broken" Cells

They are the crystalline ones that always look broken, but if they really are, then they have not been fully prepared for use. It is an extra challenge to solder wires onto them but this is how I do it: Look for the wide line on the pieces, and sort out ones that only have thin lines. The thin line ones might be useful with wire glue but are too hard to solder. Then sort the pieces with wide lines by how big they are. They will all be about 0.55 volts, but the larger pieces make more current than the smaller pieces, and it's nice to have a panel with consistent current, especially the one you make with the biggest pieces. Let's save the big pieces until we learn what to do with the small pieces. Strip apart a short length of stranded wire and put the now loose strands in a small box just so you can find them and so they don't wander into another project and cause a short circuit. Actually, another option may be to use wire-wrap wire instead of bare strands, if you don't mind stripping the end of each piece. The broken cells have a very thin conductive layer on the blue side and a very rough, thicker one on the other. It will be more challenging to solder onto them than on perfect cells but this is how. First the blue side. . .

Step 2: Preparing Broken Cells

If you can solder onto the cells then they are higher quality than the ones I have so you can skip these preparing steps. On the blue side, scratch the thick line with a very small flat screwdriver with just a little force so that the cell doesn't break, and the line should turn from white to shiny unless it's already shiny and ready to solder. Try to make a little shiny circle. We will solder there. Make the flat edge of the screwdriver completely touch the scratched area so it rubs wide. Mostly push back and forth so that the rubbing removes the thin oxidation. After scratching the line, turn the cell and scratch the circle back and forth again. Maybe turn it once more and scratch it once more. Now flip the cell over and notice the rough stuff on the back. If there appears to be two different roughnesses or shades of grey, we are going to scratch in two places. Again, turn the cell and scratch it in one or two little circles by pushing the edge of the screwdriver up and down to remove the coating that solder won't stick to. Now back to the blue side. Try to get a solder ball to stick. If it does not stick, and rosin gunks up the area, scrape it off and try again, and if it seems hopeless, scrape another part of the wide line on the cell. I did not have that problem because of practice. Now try to put a bump of solder in the two places scratched on the bottom of the cell. I was only able to get one bump to stick. There are areas on the bottom where solder just won't stick. But if neither spot sticks, try scraping the rosin off the spots and soldering again, or carefully scratching another spot. If you have a bump on the blue side, it's good but you can't lay the cell flat now. The spot that worked was rougher and thicker than the one that didn't, and that means there's a lot more silver there, and more likely it will solder.

Now that you have two solder bumps, you can attach two thin wires, either strands from stranded wire or thin wire-wrap wire. What about thicker wire? It can pull the lines off the cell and then you can forget about soldering it. Put it in the "wire glue" bin. Now that there are two wires on the cell, test it with a meter. The blue side of the cell will make up to 0.55 negative volts, so connect the meter PLUS to the wire on the silver-gray bottom of the cell. My cell isn't getting much light but the meter needle is indicating that it is making electricity.

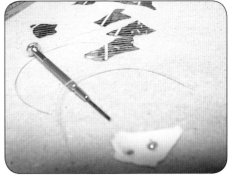

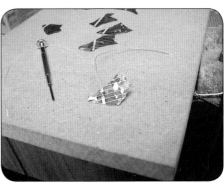

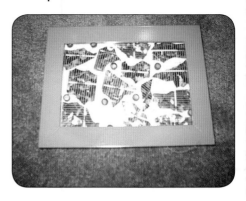

Step 4: Preparing Glass (Amorphous) Cells

Step 3: "Broken" or "Crystalline" Cell Panels

In the last step I mentioned that the blue side is negative and the silver side is positive. Now all you have to do is solder your cells in series to get more voltage. To do that you only need one more wire for each additional cell you add. Remember each cell makes up to half a volt, so consider a 12 volt panel to have 24 or more cells. A few extra is good. One reason for that is a diode lowers the voltage just a little bit, and another is that it's nice to have 12 volts for charging batteries when it's not the sunniest time of day. A diode is used when the panel charges batteries, so the batteries don't give any power back to the panel in the dark. That would be a waste of free power. Because the cells are so fragile, it would be good to install them in a deep picture frame (shadow box) with double stick foam tape or RTV glue. Be careful, this is permanent. You could make it less permanent with hot-melt glue also. At this point you don't need to think that the cells are "already broken", and you will have a well working panel. You could hide the shard-shapes with fluorescent lighting diffraction plastic over the framed panel if you like. Perhaps you've seen a shard-cell panel just like that being sold before.

I received a surplus glass cells with instructions on how to use copper mesh to make a connection to the glass cell. The glass cell was pre-scratched in the area where the mesh and wires were supposed to go. But . . . even with the copper mesh, it didn't stick. It was doable, but difficult, and not very strong. All the wires pulled off. Some of you may have had success with using copper mesh soldered to scratched areas of glass cells, but there is an easier way. Perhaps you have a broken/damaged glass cell. You may still be able to use it, unless the damage has made the glass transparent, in which case there is severe damage to the photovoltaic part of the cell. One interesting thing about the glass cells: Looking at them, you see lines, just as you may on broken or crystalline cells, but those lines are not current-collecting conductors. They are gaps between areas of the glass cell that each make about half a volt. So, glass cells can be expected to have two lines for every volt of output. And they can make 6 or 9 or 12 or 20 volts. So, we want to connect the wires to places with the most amount of lines between them to get the highest voltage. And out of the wires on the silver side, of course. Scratch the silver (probably aluminum) near the edges and test the voltage and polarity. I usually use a red wire for positive and a black or green for negative. Easy connection method: You need two brass extrusions, carefully cut with a Dremel (safety goggles!), and wires soldered on this side of the extrusions Note: The extrusion must have enough space inside it for the glass cell to fit. The extrusion is then crushed a little (before putting it on the glass) so that it will bite the glass with some pressure and make contact with the scratched edge. Slide the crushed extrusion onto the glass. If it's too crushed it won't go on, so pry it open. If it's not crushed enough it falls off, so crush it more. When it bites, and there is voltage in the light across the two extrusions, put sticky tape or just a little plastic cement over the extrusion to help it stay there. The glass cell is now ready to use. The long one shown is actually two 9-volt ones on one glass, and is the one that I put extruded contacts on because the copper mesh wouldn't stick.

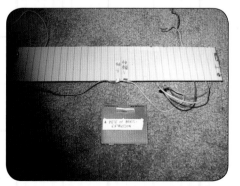

Step 5: Preparing Copper Indium Selenide Cells

These are rather well prepared already. They have easy to solder tabs and are marked which end is negative with a dash of a black marker. The ones I got, I mounted in frames and in an acrylic polymer sheet sandwich. Three in series . . . in parallel with three more in series . . . makes nice 12 volts. I have been advised that these cells undergo some kind of reaction if first exposed to full sun with no load for about 15 minutes, and that the result is good. I'm told that the result generates more output than if they are not treated this way. Just FYI. I didn't notice the difference between the panel that had pre-sunned cells and another that didn't. The cells are glass tiles that appear to be made similar to the Amorphous glass, but they are more efficient and produce around 4.5 volts and 100ma each in full sun, approximately. As they say, your mileage may vary. I have no advice for broken CIS cells. It is very easy to connect CIS cells together. Peel back the tabs a little, which point to each other under the cell, and start to peel back the sticky tape that holds it on, just enough so that you can solder them in series. And watch the polarity! I goofed it up a couple of times. No damage done, but I had to do it over. When soldering, wet the ends of the tabs with solder, then press down quickly with a popsicle stick or something to flatten them against the bottom of the cells. The cells go together nicely like tiles. With moderate carefulness, you don't need to worry much about ruining them yourself, just don't leave them alone with curious people until your panel is done and safe inside a solid frame. I've fastened them with both RTV silicone and double-sticky-foam tape. I prefer the silicone-glued result, with the cell tiles grouted against the glass from behind.

(No silicone between the cells and the frame glass.) DSFT (foam tape) is more likely to (it has, in fact) let go of a couple of the cells. As mentioned before, although I don't know if it's necessary for CIS cells, use a diode when charging batteries with the panels.

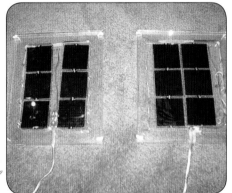

Step 6: Applications for Small Solar Panels

The solar panels I made and pictured generate around 1 or 2 watts generally. These are the applications I use them for:

- Charging batteries. In the blackout of 2003, those batteries ran our blackout party, which included black lights, fans (it was a hot day), radio, small TV, and low voltage lights. And an AC inverter. (I go to the rechargeable battery recycle bins with a meter and if they are not really dead then I borrow them until they are. I didn't buy any of these batteries.)
- Solar night lights—nowadays a very common thing where I live.
- Solar powered fans—although my solar panels run computer fans directly when it's hot (the sun makes it hot, and the sun runs the fans!), I notice that solar charged battery powered fans are *much more powerful.*
- Solar flashlights
- Solar powered radios—including my ham radio shack.

About solar-powered computers

I guess people don't leave their laptops in the sun. . . . My approach to designing a solar powered computer, (and my definition of computer is a processor with memory and a keyboard and a screen that runs not-necessarily-an-operating-system) is to use very high resistance CMOS chips, which use very little electricity, just like watches and calculators. A computer is also a calculator with lots of memory, and CMOS memory is a common thing! At nighttime, the computer has not used up all its solar power so it uses what is stored in the rechargeable battery. There is simply no demand for the solar powered computers, nor any obstacle to solar powering a PDA or a laptop with similarly sized panels.

Duty cycles

In simple theory, if you get eight hours of sun and need one hour of power, you can get by with one eighth the solar power by saving it up in batteries. Also, if LED lights should run all night, it's easy to collect more than enough solar power during the day in batteries with the right sized panel.

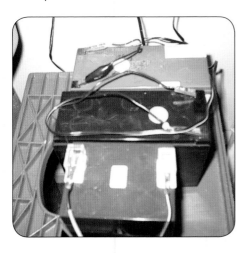

Step 7: Getting More Practical Power from Your Panel

It is very easy to get a few solar cells and put them together into a panel, but sometimes it gets expensive to get enough cells to make a useful voltage. If you obtained one or two large cells, you may have a whole watt or two, but only a volt or less, and that's sad. Not too many things run on less than a volt. Perhaps you got enough big broken cells to make 6 volts, but wouldn't it be nice to have 12 volts? Then maybe you could keep a battery charged and occasionally run an inverter on it. In the last step I mentioned how time could be used to save up power for another time when it will be used. And a small panel can make enough power over a long time to run a big load for a short time. In this step I am talking about matching the voltage of the panel, whatever it may be, to the voltage that you find useful. Or generally, matching supply and demand in a satisfying, practical way. It may be possible to design a 2 volt circuit for a 2 volt panel, but unnecessary. It is possible, only using germanium transistors as far as I know, to get any voltage out of a big half-volt cell, but I don't know a modern way, so I'll leave that idea alone. But there are many voltage doubler or multiplier circuits that work at slightly higher voltages, and I've made a few panels around 6 volts, which I'd like to get 12 out of. There is a voltage doubler chip still available called ICL7660 or MAX1044 that is very convenient to use. So I will use it as an example, since I'd rather have around a watt at 12 volts than at 6 volts. There is something else I did that was very obvious in the picture for step 1, where I had three broken cell panels around 6 volts and put them in series to get around 18 volts . . . and since the cells were large, that array has a lot of current. But if I use just one 6 volt panel and want 12 volts, I use the voltage doubler and get twice the voltage in exchange for half the current. AC transformers do the same thing . . . almost the same power goes out as goes in, but at a more useful voltage. Some circuits that do this are called "DC to DC converters".

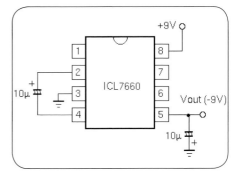

Solar Lawn Mower!

By marsh
(www.instructables.com/id/Solar-
Lawn-Mower-1/)

I've had battery powered lawn mowers before and they are a real pain to keep charged. You have to either plug them in or take the battery out and that sucks.

This is one solution to the problem. Install solar panels on the mower and just leave it parked in the sun to charge it.

Here's how I did it!

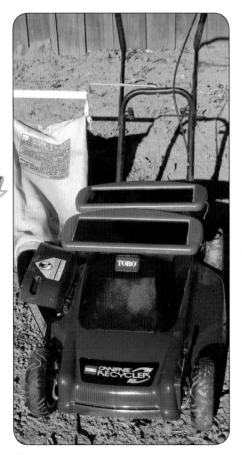

Tools and Materials Needed

Tools
- soldering iron
- wire stripper
- volt meter
- screwdriver
- wrenches

Materials
- battery-powered lawnmower
- (2)12 volt photovoltaic solar panels
- 4 general purpose rectifier diodes
- double-stick tape
- nuts, bolts, and washers
- solder

Step 1: Evaluate the Lawnmower's Current Condition

I had a DR Neuton Mower, but this Toro came up on Freecycle (www.freecycle.org). It was way more mondo than the DR, so I decided it would be the donor machine.

The first thing I did was check the batteries. They were toast, so I had to build a new battery pack.

I got four replacement batteries at my local electronic supply for $18.00 each. To keep them as a cohesive pack, I applied double-stick tape between each battery, just like the original setup had.

Step 2: How to Wire It Up

A photovoltaic (PV) solar cell has a power output recognized in watts. When the sun is shining, the potential of the PV cell is greater than that of the batteries, so energy will flow from the PV cells to the batteries.

But what happens when the sun goes down? Then the batteries have a greater potential. That means that if you don't take steps to prevent it, energy will flow

from the batteries to the PV cells. This energy will be wasted as heat emanated from the PV cells, ultimately burning them out and draining the batteries.

We can prevent this by installing diodes in the circuit. A diode is like a one-way check valve for electricity. It makes it possible for the solar panel to charge the battery, but impossible for the battery to heat the solar panel.

The circuit below shows the typical wiring for this type of application. This system uses four 6 volt batteries and is charged by two 12 volt solar panels. The overall system voltage is 24 volts. When you line up batteries, their voltage adds as you place more in the series. The panels are 12 volts so we need to isolate them from each other. The diodes also accomplish this task.

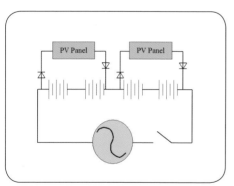

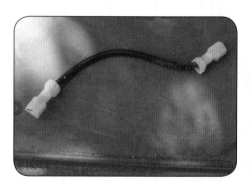

Step 3: Hook up the Batteries

Returning to the battery pack. Let's treat these four batteries as two sets of two. Hook them together as shown and test the voltage to make sure they show 12 volts per pair. OCV (open-circuit voltage) may be on the order of 14 volts. This is normal. In fact, if it's below 10 volts you may have a bad battery. Finally, there will be an interconnect between the two sets. As shown in the schematic, we need to tap this interconnect to hook up our PV cells. Do this using a wire stripper. Do not cut the wire, just breach and separate the insulation.

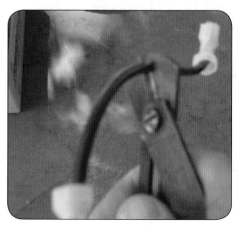

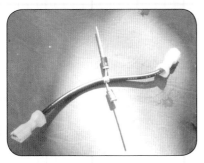

Step 4: Install the Power Taps

Just as we did on the interconnect, breach the positive power lead and install a diode. Make sure the band on the diode is closest to the red wire.

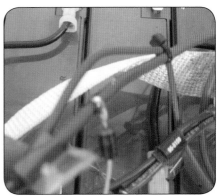

Step 5: Repeat the Process

Do the same thing again on the negative side.

This time make sure the band of the diode is facing away from the black wire.

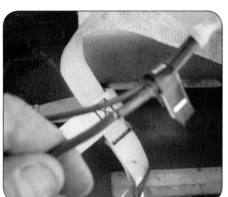

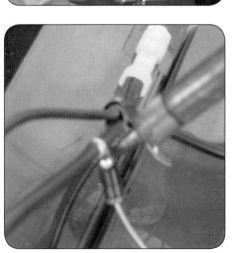

Step 6: Scavenge Some Parts

With this PV panel came a cigar lighter plug. Yes, I said cigar lighter. Read your owner's manual. That heat source is a CIGAR lighter.

We're not going to use it, but we need to take a look at it.

First, cut the PV connector off. Leave a foot or so of wire on it and strip the ends.

Set that aside and let's look at what we have left.

Open up the cigar lighter plug. There's a circuit board in there. What do you think it does?

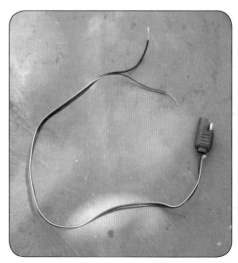

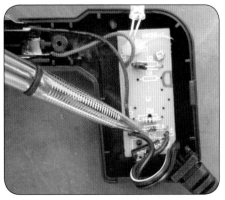

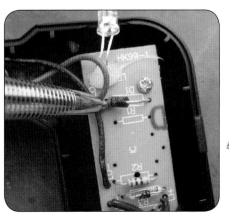

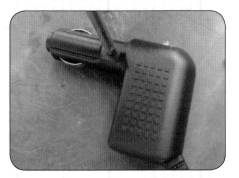

Step 7: Continuing with the Wiring

We're now ready to connect the power taps to the PV power plugs.

Slide heat shrink tubing over the wire *before* soldering the wire to the diode. Attach the wires to the diodes and solder them in place. Next, slide the shrink tubing over the solder joint and the diode and shrink it down to insulate the joint.

Make sure to get the polarity right! The stripped wire from the PV panel is positive. Make sure this wire is connected to a diode that points toward a positive terminal of the battery. I've tried to make it clear on how to make this determination.

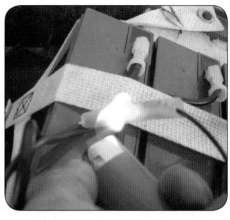

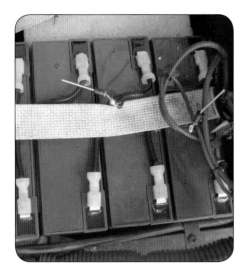

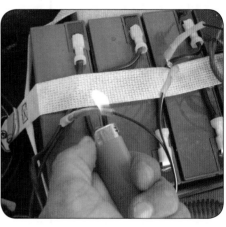

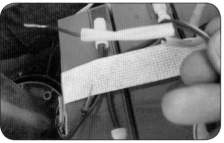

Step 8: Check Your Wiring!

At this point you should have two connectors wired through diodes to the batteries. Check these with a volt meter; there should be no voltage present. The diodes are a one-way check valve for electricity from the PV panels to the batteries, not the reverse.

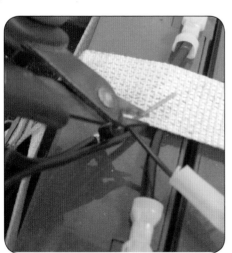

Step 9: Continue Checking Your Wiring

At this point you're all wired up and you can make some voltage checks to make sure you can safely proceed.

Step 10: Mount the PV Panels

Now that the hard part is out of the way, let's get to the easy stuff.

These panels have keyhole shaped mounting holes. Place a screw in the hole and tighten a nut down over it. This gives you a stud mounting. Align the stud onto the cover and drill mounting

holes for the PV panels. Next, cut spacers to conform to the contour of the motor cover. Don't forget, it's all plastic and the stuff flexes really well. It's pretty forgiving.

In this installation there were some reinforcements on the underside that had to be removed. Tin snips and an X-ACTO knife took care of the offending plastic pretty quickly.

Use the other half of the contour-cut spacer to shim the bottom of the mounting.

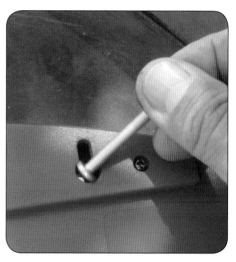

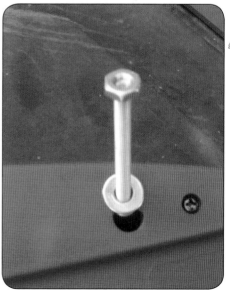

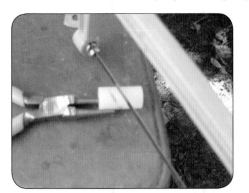

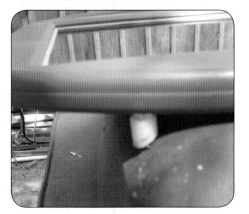

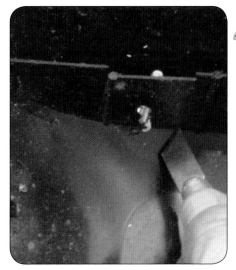

Step 11: Run the Wiring

Now that the PV panels are mounted, run the wires into the motor cover.

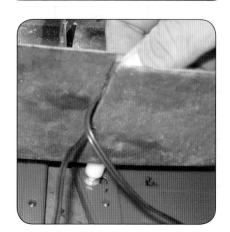

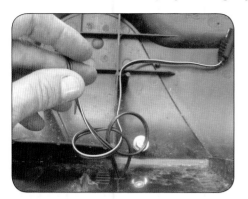

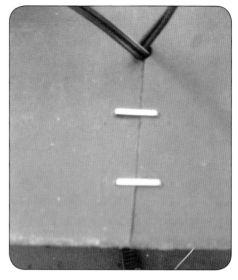

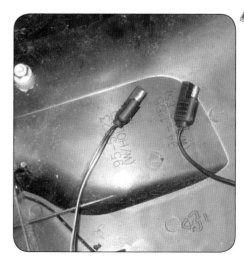

Step 12: Check the Solar Panel Output

OCV (open-circuit voltage) of these PV panels is on the order of 16 to 20 volts. If it is especially light out, this is the reading you should get.

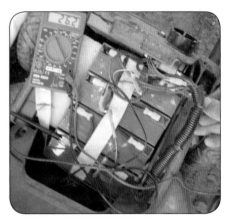

Step 14: There It Is!

It works and really works well. I've been mowing my lawn every day for three days and the mower is fully charged every time I turn it on. All I need now is a lawn.

Step 13: The Final Hookup!

Connect the PV panels to the battery banks.

Next, check your voltages. You should have two banks of 12 to 15 volts and the overall voltage should be at least 24 volts.

Solar-Powered Fountain/Herb Garden

By James Harrigan
(sleighbedguy)
(www.instructables.com/id/Solar-powered-fountainherb-garden/)

- 4" ABS pipe (2' segment)
- 4" end caps
- (2) 3/8" vinyl tubing
- shrink tubing
- wire
- epoxy
- ABS pipe cement

Tools
- drill
- saw (handsaw, band saw, jigsaw, or miter saw)
- router (useful)
- lathe (optional)

Here is a simple garden fountain utilizing a $20 solar panel/pump combo, some sewer pipe, bamboo, and a strawberry pot. The fountain will only run in direct sunlight, but the herbs will thrive in the same conditions. This one isn't hard to do, and again doesn't require any special tools. Everything should run you about $50.

Gather the Materials
- floating solar fountain (from Harbor Freight Tools)
- bamboo
- clear spray lacquer
- strawberry pot

109

Step 1: Disassemble the Fountain

This is waterproof and, therefore, taking it apart is a bit of a pain. In my case, Harbor Freight sent the wrong item as a replacement and I do not have a pool . . . so this was my only option. Flip over the fountain. Along the bottom are circular bumps. Drill through each one with room to spare. If this does not loosen it, you will have to cut the two halves apart. Your reward for this arduous task will be a pump and two solar panels. This was the by far the hardest step!

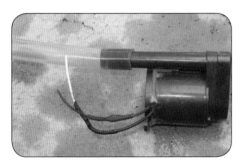

Step 2: Cut the Pipe and Bamboo

The fountain does not need to utilize bamboo, I just *really* like it. Cut the bamboo to the height you want. The fountain is supposed to have 19.5 inches of lift. Remember the water is traveling from the bottom of the pot. Measure the pipe with one cap on. After the two halves are dry-fitted, it should fit like it does in the picture below. I used a band saw, so I haven't provided a measurement. The pot might be different, and we all know no one can just draw a straight line around a cylinder. This might be a bit of trial and error. The bamboo I chose to use has the nifty little spout. This was cut on the band saw, then the horrible cut was covered with twine (epoxied in place) to hide the flaws. The sewer caps are $6 a piece, and I glued the top on first. I chose to save the $6 and make the project harder. The caps

are also domed, so I routed a small trough near the edge and drilled some drainage holes to capture most of the water. Due to another one of my mistakes, I had to make the plug to hold the bamboo upright. This isn't necessary. If you don't have a lathe, the large hole will need to fit the end of your bamboo. Or you can epoxy the bamboo to the cap. Just remember to drill for the wire and the tubing. I left out the wiring/solar panel portion. There are only two wires. Be sure to use the shrink tubing to make sure the wires are fairly well protected from the water.

around the edges of the pipe to keep the water from draining off as quickly. It has been two days, and the water is getting to the plants, but keeping the fountain running. For the solar panels, I chose to use the part of the fountain already containing everything just because it was easier than building another setup. If you do plan to make your own container for the solar panels, use super glue and clear acrylic. I did some tests with this, and it works very well.

Step 3: Dry Fitting

Assemble the fountain without gluing anything in place. If you use the a plug to hold the bamboo upright as I did, make sure the wire and tubing clear the cap and that the wire can get out of the pot. Another issue I found with my original configuration was that the spout was too long. I had to cut it nearly in half. It is better to find this out before it is totally assembled! If everything fits, lacquer up the bamboo and twine. When it's dry, you're all set.

Step 4: Plant Those Herbs and Enjoy

Some contrasting rocks hide the ABS pipe and really cap off the whole fountain. I had to add some clear vinyl

Solar PV Tracker
By bwitmer
(www.instructables.com/id/Solar-PV-tracker/)

For a class project, I decided to try making a low cost PV (photovoltaic) tracker. Being able to follow the sun's path through the sky can raise your solar panel system's output considerably (30 to 50 percent), but the argon filled ones can be a bit pricey, and seem to be a bit unsteady in wind. I looked at several different designs, looked at what materials I could find, and this is how I did it. The panel is mounted to a frame, which is attached to two bike wheels. The wheels are mounted to a larger wooden frame, and the wheels and panel are moved by a 12 volt linear actuator. The sensor is an LED model and is purchased from Redrok Energy. The LED sensor senses the path of the sun and tells the actuator how much to move to keep the panel properly oriented. At the front of the tracker are two legs that can be adjusted to the proper altitude for seasonal changes. I used bicycle wheels because they are durable, strong enough to handle some weight, and, best of all, in my case, free!

with satisfaction. Here is a picture of the top wheel being mounted.

What do You Need?

Here is what I used to make this tracker, and where everything was obtained:

- Several treated 2 × 4s (Lowes)
- Two wheels from a free bicycle (free or almost free bikes are pretty easy to find from the local landfill or thrift store)
- A piece of angle iron with pre-punched holes (Lowes)
- A 12 volt linear actuator (~$75 from eBay)
- An LED tracking sensor (~$40 from www.redrok.com/led3xassm. htm#led3xforsale)
- Various nuts, bolts, screws, cable, and wire (scrounging around my workshop)

Step 1: Making the Base and Mounting the Wheels

To make a nice, sturdy base I cut the 2 × 4s at angles and put them together to make two triangles. You can make them whatever size you need, depending on the size of your panels. I then tied them together with a couple of 2 × 4s at the base, and a couple up top. This made a nice, sturdy base to mount the wheels to. I cut a couple of small pieces of angle iron with a hacksaw, found the mid-point on the cross members, and attached them with exterior woodscrews. I put the wheels through the holes, and spun them

Step 2: Adding the Wooden Frame to the Wheels

I then mounted the 2 × 6 piece to the bike wheels by drilling holes through the bike rims and the 2 × 6 and bolting them together. I also used big U-bolts to clamp the rims to the board by drilling holes through the board and clamping it down tight. The board pivoted nicely on the two bike rims. The 2 × 6 isn't wide enough to mount the panel to, so I added some smaller 2 × 4s to the top and bottom of

113

the board, cut to the size of the panel. Each 2 × 4 board is as long as the solar panel is wide, and was attached to each end of the 2 × 6 with screws and bolts. This allows a nice flat place on which to mount the panel. I attached small pieces of angle iron to the holes on the end of each panel, and then screwed them to the wooden frame. This secured the panel to the frame.

Step 3: Adding the Linear Actuator

I purchased the 12 volt linear actuator on eBay. It's built to hold up in the weather, is strong enough to move however many panels I would want to add to it, and has a long enough stroke to move the panels all the way from one side to another. I mounted it on the one side of the frame with a through bolt and attached it to the movable solar panel frame. To mount it to the side of the frame holding the solar panel, I just used a staple on the board that moves on the bicycle wheels. A short piece of cable goes through the hole on the linear actuator and the staple, and I used a small cable clamp to secure it. This

allows everything to move around and flex as needed when it's moving. When hooked to the battery the actuator moves the panel all the way to one side and, reversing it, moves it all the way back. The next step is giving the tracker the smarts to know when and how much to move.

Step 4: Adding the LED Tracker

I wish I had more pictures of the LED tracking unit, but there is plenty of info at Redroks website. The unit uses LEDs to measure the position of the sun and tells the linear actuator how much to move and where to position the panel.

It's really a slick little unit, and at a great price. I mounted mine by putting it in an empty peanut butter jar and mounting it to a 2 × 4. I attached the 2 × 4 to the side of the unit to get the LED tracker up above the panel to give it an unobstructed view of the sun.

Step 5: Finishing It Up

This is pretty much the finished product, and it works well. I had an issue of condensation accumulating inside the peanut butter jar and had to seal it better. The size of the tracker can be made to fit however many panels you need, and there are many ways to configure a tracker like this.

Greenhouse from Old Windows

By Michael Taeuber (cheft)
(www.instructables.com/
id/Greenhouse-From-Old-
Windows/)

This is a brief guide on how I took some old windows from houses they were tearing down in my neighborhood and turned them into a small greenhouse in my backyard. I collected the windows over the course of a year and a half and the build took about three months, spending one day a week on it. I spent about $300 for the lumber for the frame and screws, caulk, latches, etc. That's almost 10 percent of what a greenhouse kit would cost. The size I built was 7 feet high × 10 feet deep × 6 feet wide. But the size of your greenhouse will depend on your windows and the time you want to put into the project.

Step 1: Collect Windows and Plan Two Pair of Equal Sides

Look for old windows and save every one you get. After you have many, lay them out and play a game trying to make two pairs of "walls" both the same height. Two to three inches won't matter as you can cover the difference with wood. Smaller holes will need to have glass cut for them or filled with something else. Keep in mind that one end will need a door and the other a hole for a fan.

Step 2: Create a Frame

Using the windows you chose as a guide, construct a frame for each wall. Use good lumber for this, as it is the structure that holds all the weight. I used all 2 × 4s for the studs and 4 × 4s for the corner posts. Choose a length that allows at least 14 inches of the stud to be placed in the ground for support.

Step 3: Brace the Walls

Start placing the walls up, bracing them well so they don't fall over. Be sure to check that they are level.

Step 4: Make the Foundation Secure

To avoid certain problems with pesky city building permits, I built the structure shed height and did not pour a concrete foundation. Instead I buried cinder blocks to stabilize the 4 × 4 corner posts. They keep it from moving an inch.

117

Step 5: Screw on Windows

I used some nice coated deck screws to affix the windows to the frame. This will allow for easy removal and replacement if any break. This side facing the camera has the empty window for a fan.

Step 6: Get a Floor

I was able to find someone who needed rocks removed from their yard. Using rocks or stones is good for two reasons: good drainage and heat storage.

Step 7: Build the Roof

This was tricky. I ended up getting siding from an old shed someone had torn down. Any material you use, look for lightweight and waterproof material. Be sure that you have some that will open for ventilation, at least 20 to 30 percent of your floor space. You can get by with less if you use a fan for ventilation. Also build the slant roof with at least a 4-degree pitch, otherwise rain may not sheet off well.

Step 8: Add the Shelves and Fans

I found an old picnic bench and this fan and shelf in the garbage. I figured I could use them in my greenhouse and save them from a landfill.

Step 9: Caulk and Paint

Use a good outdoor caulk and seal all the cracks and holes between the windows. Paint the wood to protect it from the weather.

Step 10: Winter

One winter was especially bad near me. We had several feet of snow weeks on end. Luckily, I had already emptied the greenhouse and removed the roof panels in late November. I live in a zone five area. During the last month I brought out an electric heater to keep the temperature more consistent overnight.

Later I was able to obtain a large picture window and decided to install a windowed roof in the spring. It will allow much more light in and therefore heat. I used the same deck screws to affix the windows to the roof frame I already had built. For the roof vents, I took two windows and screwed them together. I found old door hinges and used a piece of PVC as a brace. I added a screw holding it to the frame as a cotter pin. Lastly, in case a huge gust of wind came along and tried to yank open the windows, I nailed a small chain to the frame and window to prevent the window slamming backwards onto the rest of the roof.

I also modified the south facing bench. It connects to the frame on one end and still uses cinder blocks on the other. This will hopefully allow me to utilize the space inside better. It's filling quickly!

Now that the roof will allow so much light through, cooling will be a greater issue this summer. I may place some of the old panels back up in July or August to reflect some of that light. I also obtained some reflecting fabric.

Lastly, I think in the future, I will completely rebuild the roof, using the windows for a gable type structure. It will force me to use some sort of poly material to cover up the gable ends. The current pitch of the roof is not enough to slope water off the windows completely.

Step 11: Fan Window

I was unhappy with having to remove the fan/vent window and having to prop it against something while cooling the greenhouse during the day. The frame was already designed to fit the window into it. I decided to have it slide up and be held in place. I started by salvaging some hinges from an old entertainment center. They are the kind that sit completely outside the door. Plus these had a unique shape that fit around a right angle. This allowed the wooden "stops" to swing in place and hold the window up while I was venting or when the fan is in place. Across the frame I nailed some boards to hold the fan window against the frame. Lastly, I found an old pulley and fastened it to the window so I can pull it up easily.

Step 12: Spring Roof Vent Upgrades

Had a major score! A local community greenhouse was torn down and replaced. I was able to get some great parts. Here is a picture of the new window system. It originally opened the windows on the side of the greenhouse. The wheel is turned and rotates the gear attached to the pipe, opening the windows, which makes opening and shutting easy. While every window now must be open at the same time, I can control the angle at which they are open.

Also pictured is a gutter claimed from the trash. The hinge side of the roof windows always leaked profusely. The gutter catches the water and stores it in a bucket for easy watering.

Step 13: Spring Shading

Bought some secondhand rolling shades that are working great. They easily roll up and down the south facing wall while not taking up too much room.

Step 14: Winter Two Years Later

Here is the greenhouse in a mild winter. I overwinter many potted perennials inside. To insulate the roof, I stretch a sheet of poly across the top to keep out the drafts. Last October, I repainted both the inside and out. All the wood is doing well. I hope that, with care, the greenhouse will last over ten years. It has changed the way I garden, making my backyard much more productive.

An Algae Bioreactor from Recycled Water Bottles

By Michael H. Fischer
(mfischer)
(www.instructables.com/id/An-Algae-Bioreactor-from-Recycled-Water-Bottles/)

In this Instructable, we describe how to build a photo-bioreactor that uses algae to convert carbon dioxide and sunlight into energy. The energy that is produced is in the form of algae biomass. The photo-bioreactor is built from plastic recycled water bottles. By designing the apparatus to be compartmentalized, we are able to do many experiments in parallel. By using algae as a biofuel, we can increase the world's supply of oil while at the same time we decrease the amount of atmospheric carbon dioxide used during its production. The resulting product is a sustainable biofuel whose carbon footprint is neutral inasmuch as the CO_2 produced on consumption is essentially balanced by the CO_2 used in its production. In this Instructable, we first make the carbon dioxide delivery system, then mount the water bottles on a rack, and then inoculate the bottles with algae. After letting the algae grow for a week, we extract the biomass.

Step 1: Make Carbon Dioxide Delivery System

To make the carbon dioxide delivery system, connect an eight-port sprinkler system manifold to a 1" long PVC pipe. To get good seals, use Teflon tape to tape the threads before attaching the pieces together. Next, attach the 1" pipe to a T-connector. Block off one end of the T-connector and attach the other end to 1' long PVC pipe.

Step 2: Attach Tubing to Manifold

For each manifold, cut eight pieces of flexible tubing and connect each piece to a port of the manifold. The manifold that I am using has a dial on each port to control the rate of flow. Make sure all the ports that you use are open and allow approximately the same amount of carbon dioxide to flow through the port.

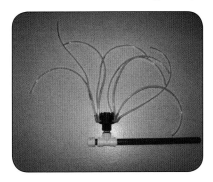

Step 3: Mount Carbon Dioxide System

Mount the air system to a metal rack using zip ties. Attach the air system to a tank of carbon dioxide.

Step 4: Mount Water Bottles

Hot glue the water bottles to the metal rack.

Step 5: Make Algae Media

We next make the medium to grow the algae. Although there are many possible mediums, a standard garden store fertilizer contains all the nitrogen and nutrients that the algae need.

Step 6: Media Inoculation

A good source of algae is pond algae, if available. If not, there are a large number of online vendors that sell batches of algae. To inoculate the culture, measure out a fixed amount of algae and add it to the growth medium.

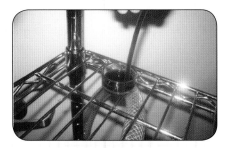

extract the algae from the solution. The biomass of the dried algae can then be used as a fuel. As a by-product of this process, a large amount of atmospheric CO_2 is sequestered.

Step 7: Growth and Harvesting

After several days of sunlight and CO_2 exposure, the algae are much denser. A French press is then used to

CONVERSION TABLES

One person's inch is another person's centimeter. Instructables projects come from all over the world, so here's a handy reference guide that will help keep your project on track.

Measurement								
	1 Millimeter	1 Centimeter	1 Meter	1 Inch	1 Foot	1 Yard	1 Mile	1 Kilometer
Millimeter	1	10	1,000	25.4	304.8	—	—	—
Centimeter	0.1	1	100	2.54	30.48	91.44	—	—
Meter	0.001	0.01	1	0.025	0.305	0.91	—	1,000
Inch	0.04	0.39	39.37	1	12	36	—	—
Foot	0.003	0.03	3.28	0.083	1	3	—	—
Yard	—	0.0109	1.09	0.28	033	1	—	—
Mile	—	—	—	—	—	—	1	0.62
Kilometer	—	—	1,000	—	—	—	1.609	1

Volume									
	1 Milliliter	1 Liter	1 Cubic Meter	1 Teaspoon	1 Tablespoon	1 Fluid Ounce	1 Cup	1 Pint	1 Quart	1 Gallon
Milliliter	1	1,000	—	4.9	14.8	29.6	—	—	—	—
Liter	0.001	1	1,000	0.005	0.015	0.03	0.24	0.47	0.95	3.79
Cubic Meter	—	0.001	1	—	—	—	—	—	—	0.004
Teaspoon	0.2	202.9	—	1	3	6	48	—	—	—
Tablespoon	0.068	67.6	—	0.33	1	2	16	32	—	—
Fluid Ounce	0.034	33.8	—	0.167	0.5	1	8	16	32	—
Cup	0.004	4.23	—	0.02	0.0625	0.125	1	2	4	16
Pint	0.002	2.11	—	0.01	0.03	0.06	05	1	2	8
Quart	0.001	1.06	—	0.005	0.016	0.03	0.25	.05	1	4
Gallon	—	0.26	264.17	0.001	0.004	0.008	0.0625	0.125	0.25	1

conversion tables

Mass and Weight						
	1 Gram	1 Kilogram	1 Metric Ton	1 Ounce	1 Pound	1 Short Ton
Gram	1	1,000	—	28.35	—	—
Kilogram	0.001	1	1,000	0.028	0.454	—
Metric Ton	—	0.001	1	—	—	0.907
Ounce	0.035	35.27	—	1	16	—
Pound	0.002	2.2	—	0.0625	1	2,000
Short Ton	—	0.001	1.1	—	—	1

Speed		
	1 Mile per hour	1 Kilometer per hour
Miles per hour	1	0.62
Kilometers per hour	1.61	1

Temperature		
	Fahrenheit (°F)	Celsius (°C)
Fahrenheit	—	(°C x 1.8) + 32
Celsius	(°F − 32) / 1.8	—

Notes for your projects

notes

also available

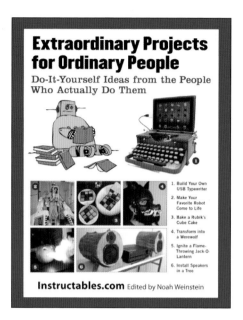

Collected in this volume is a best-of selection from Instructables, reproduced for the first time outside of the web format, retaining all of the charm and ingenuity that make Instructables such a popular destination for internet users looking for new and fun projects designed by real people in an easy-to-digest way.

Hundreds of Instructables are included, ranging from practical projects like making a butcher block counter top or building solar panels to fun and unique ideas for realistic werewolf costumes or transportable camping hot tubs. The difficulty of the projects ranges from beginner on up, but all are guaranteed to raise a smile or a "Why didn't I think of that?"

Numerous full-color pictures accompany each project, detailing each step of the process along the way. It's an invitation to try a few yourself, and once you're done, see if you don't have a couple of ideas to share at Instructables.com.

US $16.95 paperback ISBN: 978-1-62087-057-0

also available

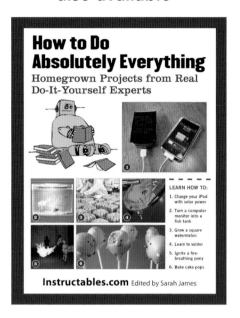

How to Do Absolutely Everything
Homegrown Projects from Real Do-It-Yourself Experts

LEARN HOW TO:
1. Charge your iPod with solar power
2. Turn a computer monitor into a fish tank
3. Grow a square watermelon
4. Learn to solder
5. Ignite a fire-breathing pony
6. Bake cake pops

Instructables.com Edited by Sarah James

Continuing the Instructables series with Skyhorse Publishing, a mammoth collection of projects has been selected and curated for this special best-of volume of Instructables. The guides in this book cover the entire spectrum of possibilities that the popular website has to offer, showcasing how online communities can foster and nurture creativity.

From outdoor agricultural projects to finding new uses for traditional household objects, the beauty of Instructables lies in their ingenuity and their ability to find new ways of looking at the same thing. *How to Do Absolutely Everything* has that in spades; the possibilities are limitless, thanks to not only the selection of projects available here, but also the new ideas you'll build on after reading this book. Full-color photographs illustrate each project in intricate detail, providing images of both the individual steps of the process and the end product.

US $16.95 paperback ISBN: 978-1-62087-066-2